The English Reformation

Studymates

Many other titles in preparation

The English Reformation

The Effect on a Nation

Dr Andrew Chibi

www.studymates.co.uk

First published in 2004 by Studymates Limited, PO Box 2, Bishops Lydeard, Somerset TA3 3YE, United Kingdom

Telephone: (01823) 432002
Fax: (01823) 430097

Typeset by PDQ Typesetting, Newcastle-under-Lyme
Printed and bound in Great Britain

Contents

Author's Preface

Although writing seems a very solitary pursuit, authors rapidly accumulate many debts, which need acknowledgement. Writing this kind of academic textbook garnered several intellectual arrears. To former students who asked the right questions at the right time, forcing me to think about the answers. Their actual names might now escape me (my students have learned to suffer my bad memory), but they attended my lectures, seminars and tutorials at Southampton, Manchester Metropolitan, Leicester and Trinity and All Saints College. As usual, Mark Greengrass, Terry Hartley and Peter Musgrave gave me inspiration, advice and support. Ian Campbell and Graham Lawler both advised me and believed in the project.

I have personal debts too. I would like to thank, Paul Shawley (who fancies himself some kind of universal grand Pooh-Bah just because he sits behind a screen and rolls dice at us to no discernable purpose ah, the value of a psychology degree), James Burtoft, David Hutchesson and Jo and Daz Johnson-Smith for dragging me away from my computer from time to time. Of course, my greatest debts are to my family, especially to my wife Ellen for her unwavering support and encouragement, and to Andy and Eleanor Chibi, George and Anne Turton, Joan, Melinda, Chris, Kevin, Rachel, Marley, Andrew, Christopher and Nicky. Last, but not least, what would I do without Jake's constant editorial commentary?

Although these people can take some credit for the appearance of this book, all mistakes, gaffes, errors and evidence of poor scholarship are entirely my own.

Andrew Allan Chibi
andrew.chibi@studymates.co.uk

Introduction

One-minute summary – 'Reformation' often alludes to sweeping religious change. In the Tudor period, this amounted to an entirely unique 'English' church (featuring both Catholic and Protestant elements) by 1603. It was not a popular movement, however – not a grass roots demand for change – but an attempt by Tudor authorities to enforce a broadly-based unifying institution. They did this to bolster security and stability. Success called for a balancing act between the needs of the crown, the state, the church and an ever increasingly pious and informed population. We shall see many options tried over the period. This introduction will help you to understand:

▶ why the Tudor Reformation needs to be studied
▶ why reformation was needed in the first place.

Why study the Tudor Reformation?

Today, especially for those of an English-speaking Christian background, religion is not very central to life. Thus, the Reformation period is often of remote interest for, indeed, what relevance could it possibly have to the modern world? Of course, this is precisely the point. Society (and the English church) is the way it is, largely because of the changes brought about under the Tudors. To understand better the modern world, we must understand how it evolved. Studying the Tudor Reformation is a giant step towards comprehension. First, some advice:

▶ be prepared to use your imagination
▶ put aside modern thoughts and preconceptions.

Church and society were not always as they are now. This may seem obvious but, for all that, it still needs to be firmly grasped before you can truly appreciate the magnitude of our topic.

Imagine a world in which the church was central to every aspect of your life. It was there at your birth, your adulthood and, under normal circumstances, a priest was the last person you saw before you died. It was at the heart of the social, economic, political, and cultural sphere of every single community. Moreover, it was also part of an international institution, owing spiritual allegiance to Rome, participating in the defence of Christendom and taking succour from the sure salvation it guaranteed. In brief, by studying the Tudor Reformation we can trace the evolutionary process from that world to the one in which we live today.

But, if the church was so ideal, why change it?
This important question has two possible answers. Either:

▶ something was wrong with it, or
▶ the political élites had a (hidden) agenda.

If it was the first, these problems should be easily identified. Moreover, we should expect to find little resistance to necessary change. If it was the second, we need to uncover what those in power wanted, and why this could not be achieved without disruption.

Was reformation necessary?

Just because it happened, do not think it was inevitable. Contemporaries did not know change was forthcoming (although some may have suspected), nor did they necessarily want it. We have to understand the reasons why those who did want change desired it, and how they brought it about.

So, what was wrong with the pre-Reformation church?
Some historians highlight 'abuses' within, and 'anti-clericalism' outside, of the church of the late fifteenth-, and early sixteenth-, centuries. Abuses such as:

▶ non-residence (when a clergyman lives elsewhere than his post)
▶ high clerical taxation (costly fees and charges)
▶ materialism (greed)
▶ pluralism (holding more than one office at the same time)
▶ simony (the buying and selling of ecclesiastical privileges solely for economic gain)
▶ nepotism
▶ ignorance (poorly educated priests).

As a result, people felt morally and spiritually insecure, at a time when personal piety and spiritual expectations were on the rise. And, as the church was at its heart, society itself was destabilising at a time when stability was desperately needed (the Wars of the Roses were not long past). We have to be careful, however, not to exaggerate these problems.

Other historians suggest that the problems were not quite so serious. Yes, there were non-resident priests but, for each one, there were thousands who were resident. For each pluralist, there were thousands who were devoted to one position. The vast majority of laymen had no grievances with their priests at all. But, we can agree that there were some problems from which men like John Colet and Simon Fish demanded solutions (you should look them up). It seems clear that such problems were not severe enough to cause the widespread discontent that we find elsewhere in

Europe so, perhaps, the second option is the better explanation.

Why did those in power need change?
Clearly, this is our central focus but, let me add two things. Long before the reign of Henry VIII, the church (centred in Rome) successfully served the needs of the English people (there had even been an English pope!). It also provided England with stability and security. By the 1530s, however, this seemed to be no longer the case and, thus, had to be reformed. Further, by examining how and why the church was changed, we can begin to understand the church and society as we now know them.

1

Henry VIII – The Break with Rome, c. 1527–1534

One-minute summary — Henry needed a 'divorce' from Catherine of Aragon and, to get it, he petitioned Rome. He wanted the issue resolved in England by loyal clergymen and threatened and whittled away at papal authority to get his way. When he failed, he cut all further ties and pursued three other policies – royal supremacy, political autonomy and secularisation of church property. This chapter will help you to understand:

▶ why the divorce was necessary and how it was achieved
▶ the role of Anne Boleyn
▶ the fall of Thomas Wolsey
▶ how to access the 'supremacy' issue
▶ the role of parliament
▶ how to assess the opposition.

Why was a 'divorce' necessary?

Strictly speaking, what Henry wanted was an 'annulment'. That is, he wanted the Pope to declare the marriage null and void. His reasons were many (and not all convincing). These include:

▶ a claim of 'incestuous cohabitation' with his brother's widow
▶ insufficient legal authority and, other unresolved questions
▶ a declining political and economic relationship with Spain
▶ a series of miscarriages and stillbirths (and that the one surviving child was female).

The last point is particularly important as it endangered the Tudor dynasty's survival.

Incestuous cohabitation?
Simply put, Henry had married his elder brother (Arthur's) widow and it could be construed that, having done so, he had transgressed divine law. On 17 May 1527, he was summoned into an ecclesiastical court, by the authority of the two highest religious authorities in England – Thomas Wolsey and William Warham – to explain himself. On 20 May, his lawyers excused the marriage by presenting Pope Julius II's bull of dispensation (the legal authority). Further objections were to have been raised on 31 May but, at this crucial point, the trial was overtaken by other events. On 6 May, Rome had been sacked by Imperial troops.

Why is this important?

Charles V, the Emperor whose troops held the Pope, Clement VII, a virtual prisoner, was also Catherine's nephew. The Pope was in no position to agree to anything that might harm his chances of freedom or hurt Habsburg pride.

Other unresolved questions

At this time, marriages, divorces and annulments were difficult to arrange. There were moral issues to consider, as well as questions of diplomacy. But, more importantly, there were issues like fertility and legal obstacles to consider. Modern concepts like love and compatibility would not have been considered important. Henry VII and Ferdinand of Aragon (Catherine's father) had arranged the marriage for their own benefit. The lack of living male children, however, was the most considerable problem.

Why is this important?

In the Tudor age, children were considered gifts from God, and if a couple could not produce a child, it was considered a divine curse. Henry, a very religious man, became obsessed by the notion that God disliked the Tudors, and asked what he could do to assuage God's anger. His book against Martin Luther (*Assertion of the Seven Sacraments*, 1518), a considerable achievement, earned him the title 'Defender of the Faith' from the Pope, but God sent him no male heirs.

He had a female heir – Princess Mary

Unfortunately, succession was only guaranteed through a prince. England had never had a queen regnant and neither social custom nor the legal system was (in theory) set up to support one. Moreover, the Wars of the Roses (fought over succession issues), were well within living memory.

You are there ...

Had you lived at this time, you or your parents may have witnessed those wars, and such outrages as the murders of two little princes (Edward and Richard), perhaps by their own uncle (Richard III). The Tudor dynasty brought peace. Would you risk further succession wars or would you support Henry in his efforts to ensure his dynasty's survival?

In brief, Henry needed a *legitimate* male heir. (Note the word 'legitimate'.)

Catherine was in her forties and so many failed pregnancies had left her barren, disfigured and not a little irritable. Now, only a miracle would save the Tudors, but one did not seem to be forthcoming. The obvious solution for Henry was to end his cursed marriage. An annulment meant it had never taken place – the curse would be removed. With the Pope incarcerated, however, getting an annulment would not be a simple matter. Even Cardinal Wolsey, Henry's problem solver, failed on this one. Through his efforts, we can trace problems in:

▶ diplomacy
▶ law
▶ theology.

Never forgetting the issue of legitimacy.

Understanding why diplomacy failed

Besides the fact of the Pope's virtual imprisonment and Catherine's familial connection to Charles V, there was a problem about where Wolsey's ultimate loyalties lay. In essence, he served two masters (King and Pope) and seemed loathe to decide between them. But, to his credit, Wolsey whittled away at the issue for two years, always indirectly, trying to find a political or legal solution:

▶ firstly by trying to have his own religious authority in England confirmed

▶ secondly by appealing to Francis I and the French cardinals to have himself declared *vice-pope* during Pope Clement's incarceration.

Seeing this, Henry wondered whether Wolsey served his King, his Pope or his own ambitions first. Moreover, his actions alerted the rest of Europe to Henry's dilemma. But, by simply allowing the Pope to 'escape' (still surrounded by troops), Charles neatly undermined Wolsey's political ambitions and any papal solutions to Henry's problem. Henry blamed Wolsey and the Pope for the delay, rather than Charles because:

▶ Clement should have acted according to the higher moral reason of curing a breach of divine law.

▶ Charles's territories included the Low Countries, the focus of the English wool trade and, therefore possible damage to the English economy.

▶ Wolsey had achieved nothing.

In desperation, Wolsey turned to a military solution. Backed by English money, French forces pushed Imperial troops out of Rome – 'freeing' the Pope and extending French influence. Thereafter, Wolsey's agents secured a *decretal commission* that allowed him to re-examine the marriage in England, but:

▶ Cardinal Lorenzo Campeggio was assigned to hear the case as senior partner to Wolsey (and had been instructed to forestall any decision);

▶ the volatile political situation forced the Pope to issue only a 'secret' commission (politically 'deniable') which Campeggio later destroyed;

▶ the second trial, at Blackfriars, was a fiasco.

Where diplomacy had failed, perhaps law would prevail?

Understanding canon law, and why the legal approach also failed

We need to re-examine those unresolved legal issues. Three serious impediments had stood between Catherine and Henry when their marriage was proposed – *affinity*, *consanguinity* and *public honesty*.

Affinity refers to the relationship (based on marriage or sexual intercourse) between a person and their partner's 'blood' relatives (which barred potential marriages to the fourth degree). In essence, a man could not marry any of his partner's relatives closer than fourth cousins (as outlined in Leviticus, Chapter 18). Through affinity, they were also his true relatives. They also become 'blood' relatives due to **consanguinity**.

Picturing the scene ...
Imagine yourself married at this time. Through affinity and consanguinity, your spouse's parents are your parents; your spouse's siblings are your siblings (you are related to these people in the first degree). You are also related to aunts/uncles-in-law, daughters/sons-in-law, etc., and cannot consider marrying any of them should your spouse die.

Marriages between people too closely related by blood (below forth cousins) were considered to be incestuous.

Henry knew this, and married Catherine (his sister-in-law) anyway. Their marriage was not considered incestuous, however, because it was thought that a papal bull nullified the sin. **Public honesty** was a man-made legality regarding the marriage contract. The couple were either promised or married and could not, therefore, marry someone else. If, however, the marriage was not subsequently consummated, the original contract could be legally overturned – it would no longer exist; the couple would be unwed. Thus, legally, the marriage would be null and void if the original bull proved inadequate on any of these issues. Luckily, this seemed to be the case:

▶ it did not seem to sufficiently address affinity and consanguinity
▶ it did not address public honesty.

The first point became the focus of Henry's lawyers as the original bull said that Catherine and Arthur had only *probably* consummated their marriage (which Catherine denied).

Even so, if a late brother's wife was within God's forbidden degrees, could a pope lawfully dispense with it? More seriously, however, by claiming non-consummation, Catherine reduced the issue to one of affinity and public honesty (which could be resolved, albeit retroactively, by another papal bull). Henry would be back to square one unless he could prove Catherine had not been a virgin when they married.

How could this be proved?

Odd as it sounds, this was not a unique dilemma. Sometimes a woman's virginity had to be proven and this involved midwives or, indeed, sheets from the wedding bed (with tell-tale bloodstains) which would have been saved for such a situation. In this case, however, the sheets from neither of Catherine's wedding nights were available. It came down to a question of whom to believe?

Catherine claimed non-consummation. Arthur, it is well documented, hinted that his marriage had been consummated, but Henry, originally, claimed Catherine had been a virgin. To later claim otherwise sounds suspicious.

Picturing the scene ...

Imagine yourself in either princes' place – as a teenage boy who knows full well that his manhood, reputation and ability to rule are on the line. Moreover, if your wife was not a virgin, there might arise a question of legitimacy if a child was born less than nine months later. What would you do? In Arthur's place, would you claim consummation? In Henry's place, would you claim virginity (at the time) and non-virginity later? The Tudor dynasty rests on your decision.

Obviously it suited both princes, in their time, to make the claims they did, but it also suited Catherine to claim that her first marriage had not been consummated. Then, she could stay in England and marry Henry without too much bother. Later, she used it as a petty revenge for the treatment she was receiving at his hands.

Picturing the scene ...

Put yourself in Catherine's place. Raised, almost from birth to consider yourself an English princess, you finally get to England and marry the prince. Little more than a year later, he dies and you are not pregnant. Unless you have something to offer, you are disposable to England and Spain alike. But, by claiming non-consummation you would leave the door open to a second marriage (to a dashing prince). After almost 20 years of constant pregnancies, dead children, faithful service and boon companionship, however, he says you were never married. Would you be angry, try to frustrate his plans, or meekly step aside, believing he was acting for England's future?

As if to muddy the waters further, Catherine now referred to a so-called 'Spanish brief'. This was, apparently, a corrected copy of the papal bull that recognised her non-consummation claim. How suspicious is it that Henry could never get the original from Spain? Ultimately, it does not matter. The Blackfriars trial of May to July 1529 resolved nothing as:

▶ a papal court, it followed the papal calendar (recessing for winter)
▶ Campeggio had been instructed to stall
▶ Campeggio accepted Catherine's appeal to Rome.

Try to imagine how angry Henry must have been (almost three years wasted).

Clearly, canon law arguments against his marriage were just not good enough and, indeed, what one bull failed to do, another could easily achieve anyway. So, while his marriage would, perhaps, no longer be cursed, he would be no closer to a legitimate male heir either. Thus, since a legal solution was not forthcoming, he decided to attack the marriage on theological grounds.

What are these?
In essence, what Henry's scholars tried to prove was that his marriage transgressed divine laws that no pope could dispense.

What is 'divine law'?
Think 'God's law' or 'natural law'. For example, the Ten Commandments are divine laws. Much of the text of Leviticus was considered divine law, having been declared by God directly. This gave Henry a foothold in theology as Aquinas himself had written that divine law was beyond papal dispensation. Thus, if the marriage contravened divine law, a papal bull was meaningless – Henry and Catherine would, in effect, have never been married.

Did it contravene divine law?
Maybe. The issue centred around two supporting biblical texts:

▶ *Leviticus 18.16*: 'You shall not uncover the nakedness of your brother's wife; she is your brother's nakedness.'

▶ *Leviticus 20.21*: 'If a man takes his brother's wife, it is impurity; he has uncovered his brother's nakedness, they shall be childless.'

Henry's men said that these citations proved that it was prohibited for a man to 'marry' his brother's widow. The queen's men counterclaimed that these opposed both marriage and sexual congress only with a 'living' brother's wife. They put forward another citation:

▶ *Deuteronomy 25.5*: 'When brethren dwell together, and one of them dies without leaving children, the wife shall not take another, but shall be taken by the brother, and raise up seed to his brother.'

Catherine's scholars claimed that this proved that, indeed, the brother must 'marry' his widowed sister-in-law. Henry's men opined, instead, that it meant merely that a brother should provide his widowed sister-in-law with a child in his brother's name. Of course, both sides found supporting evidence:

▶ in countless biblical and spiritual texts
▶ in other theological sources (the ancient Fathers or other scholars).

Each made further rhetorical and intellectual claims.

What can non-theologians make of all this?

Consider consanguinity, and take 'uncover the nakedness' to mean 'intercourse'. Now, read Leviticus 18.16 and 20.21 again. It seems now to outlaw sex with your sister-in-law (she is your sister), whether your brother is alive or not. But, was this also, as Henry's men claimed, a bar to marriage? Well, consider the result that '... they shall be childless'. If the queen's men were correct, then would the fact of no resulting children – from otherwise adulterous sex – be much of a penalty? Now consider Deuteronomy 25:5, especially the words '... take' and '... shall be taken'. Henry's men said that this meant only intercourse. In other words, a brother's moral obligation to impregnate his widowed sister-in-law. Odd? Yes, but it is an important point.

In brief, Deuteronomy advocates an ancient Jewish custom called the '*levirate*'. In ancient times, when the Jewish tribes were dispersed, it was important that wealth and property remain within the confines of the tribe or, indeed, the family. A man needed an heir (preferably male) lest his property be lost or dispersed. If a man died without an heir, his wife and brother, to safeguard his property, would produce one for him. The brother, however, had his own wife with whom to produce his own heirs. It was an unpopular practice, had died out long before Henry's time, and applied only to Jews.

So, it seems that Henry had illicitly married his dead brother's wife and had been cursed as a result. He now only needed a competent, legitimate religious authority to recognise this, and he would be free. Lest we forget Catherine's side, however, let us recap what we already know. She claimed two things:

▶ to have been a virgin when she married Henry
▶ that a corrected copy of the original bull confirmed this.

If true, they were related only in affinity terms (easily dispensed by another bull). Her scholars said Leviticus referred only to a living brother (not to marriage) and that Deuteronomy superseded it anyway (coming later in the Bible). Much depends, of course, on whether you believe Catherine or not, and add this to established custom.

Pope Julius II *had* dispensed with the impediments to the marriage and the bull *had been used*. Other popes had issued similar bulls in the past and no one had complained, so legal precedent was on Catherine's side. Moreover, taking the citations together would seem to imply that God had ordered a man to act illicitly – which, obviously, could not be the case. Thus, Leviticus and Deuteronomy had to be read in such a way as to remove the apparent paradox. For Catherine, therefore, Leviticus would apply, except in the one case outlined in Deuteronomy (conveniently matching her own). Let us now consider another complication – Anne Boleyn.

The influence of Anne Boleyn

Was she:

▶ an ambitious harridan?
▶ the pawn of a politically ambitious faction of nobles?
▶ the tool of a politically ambitious family?
▶ a witch?
▶ all, none, or some of the above?

Had she really been coached to attract Henry's attention but not to give in to his sexual advances until they were married? The Boleyns moved cautiously because Anne's sister Mary had been Henry's mistress. She was later married off to a courtier – a comfortable life, but one that had afforded her family no political gains. It is logical to assume that the Boleyn family wanted more. Anne would become queen, but did Henry go through six years of trouble merely because he desired her sexual favours?

How much real influence did she have?
She clearly had some influence, but we must not exaggerate it. Henry wanted to marry her even though she was also related to him within proscribed degrees of affinity and consanguinity (through Mary Boleyn). But, did withholding her sexual favours drive Henry to greater efforts to rid himself of his aged and barren wife? Or is there more to it? Again, you must decide for yourself, but consider three points:

▶ Henry's sexual mores
▶ the nature of Henry's court
▶ Henry's stated needs and desires.

Understanding Henry's sexual mores
In Henry's day, kings had mistresses. His contemporaries, Francis I and Charles V, had several. And being a royal mistress had its advantages, such as:

- social power and influence at court
- the possibility of advantageous marriages to leading courtiers.

Moreover, kings fathered illegitimate children. James IV of Scotland had many, as did Francis I. Henry, however, had only one (Henry Fitzroy). Thus, he appears to have been quite moral; his religious scruples were stronger than his sexual urges.

Understanding the style of Henry's court

If you recall what you know of chivalry, if only stories about King Arthur and the Knights of the Round Table, then you will have a fair picture of the kind of romantic renaissance court Henry liked to encourage. He liked frequent jousts, masques and balls, and he encouraged secret admirers and the exchange of tokens, love letters and poems. He liked such games because he wanted his court to reflect continental cultures. Anne, raised and trained at the court of Francis I, also liked these games. Placed in this context (his religious scruples understood), do Henry's love letters, exchanges of tokens and vows of undying love for Anne evince sexual frustration, or chivalric romance?

Understanding Henry's stated needs and desires

What do we know?

- Henry needed a legitimate male heir.
- Only Mary had survived childhood.
- God cursed transgressions of divine law.

Henry's marriage seemed to be cursed. He must rid himself of Catherine and find a wife (with whom he could produce a son). But, the son had to be 'legitimate' – there could be no question marks over his birth. Henry had to be absolutely sure that every avenue had been pursued to exhaustion before he acted on his own authority. As a good, moral Catholic, he focused most on a religious solution. Therefore what can we conclude?

- he needed a legitimate male heir
- sex outside of marriage would produce only a bastard child.

He could not risk impregnating Anne until they could be legally married. (It took six years.)

Picturing the scene...
Put yourself in Henry's place. You need a legitimate male heir, fear the potential of illicit intercourse, but very much enjoy the trappings of chivalry. Pledging eternal love is acceptable, but it could go no further. Would you risk dynastic success and England's well being for mere sex?

Assessing the resolution

We have considered much – canon law, moral custom, dynastic need, theology, diplomacy, sex – and found one fact – Henry needed a legitimate male heir. To assess the resolution then, we must assess the value of everything around that fact. On 23 May 1533, at the Priory of St Peter at Dunstable, Thomas Cranmer reviewed the evidence and declared the marriage null and void. Apparently, Henry's theologians were right. To Cranmer:

▶ the royal marriage was contrary to divine law
▶ the Pope could not dispense divine law.

What about the Deuteronomy/Leviticus paradox?
Henry's scholars had turned this to their advantage by showing that God had ordered men to commit sins elsewhere:

▶ *Genesis 22.2* – Abraham was ordered to kill his son.
▶ *Judges 16.28–30* – Samson was ordered to commit suicide.

He claimed the implicit sin could be removed by God (at least for a time). God alone could order a contradiction. But, as Henry had no such divine orders, his marriage had been cursed. Since a pope could not dispense divine law, his marriage had never been legitimate.

Understanding the break with Rome

Briefly putting aside Cranmer's judgement, the ongoing saga of the 'divorce', and the continual delay of a satisfactory conclusion, illustrated two ideas:

▶ the undesirability of any form of foreign influence (as both king and country had been denied critical needs such as the annulment by foreigners)

▶ the court of Rome was corrupt (petty politics and errors in judgement may have harmed the Tudor dynasty).

Henry began to think about history. As with the divorce, were there other instances where popes had erred or claimed too much authority? Could further association potentially undermine royal authority? How could undivided loyalty from his subjects, or his power over them, be guaranteed? If papal authority was set aside, could he still get a legitimate male heir? Considerations on such issues fostered three further movements:

- anti-clericalism
- caesaro-papist theory
- parliamentary schemes.

Understanding anti-clericalism

In essence, this refers to any negative opinion about the clergy.

As stated before, the church was central to almost everyone's day-to-day existence. At the parish level, the priest was the dominant figure in the community and, generally, the only link between the laity and the wider kingdom. The church conditioned almost all other social and cultural ideas. A priest stood between God and man, representing one to the other. In general, people were satisfied with this, provided there were no, too obvious, abuses of clerical authority. Of course, problems existed, including:

- simony
- nepotism
- non-residence and pluralism
- sexual incontinence.

(See 'Summary of key ideas' at the end of this chapter.) Moreover, priests were sometimes accused of ignorance (of Latin or of basic theology) and of arrogance. Some malcontents even pointed to the vast economic disparity between themselves and some clergymen and asked how it was justifiable.

You are there ...

Imagine yourself living at the time. You are probably poor, farming the lands of a rich noble. You suffer through drought, hard winters, plagues. Your priest, who seems no better educated than you, seems to suffer less and may be living suspiciously well. How could he possibly understand the pains and torments of your life, when he suffers none? Would you begin to develop a negative opinion of him or have you already done so?

It is important to remember that only a very small percentage of clergymen abused their privileges. In the short term, however, that was enough to justify a reaction.

Assessing the reaction

Henry wanted to capitalise on what little anti-clericalism existed in order to pursue three roughly interlocking policy objectives:

- to discredit Wolsey
- to reduce clerical power via parliamentary legislation
- to discredit other high profile clergymen.

Why he wanted these will be explained later.

Understanding Wolsey's downfall

The cardinal seemed to personify everything negative. At one point, he was archbishop of York, bishop of Winchester, Durham and Bath and Wells simultaneously. Worse then this, even, he had failed the king. His downfall, therefore, tells us a great deal:

▶ other English churchmen would fear Henry's wrath
▶ the Pope could not save Wolsey (so he could not save the English churchmen either)
▶ Henry would brook no divided loyalties.

Note that Wolsey had submitted to Henry's authority through the court of King's Bench. While thus avoiding the consequences of a parliamentary *attainder* (which might have meant death), he also gave tacit recognition of Henry's authority over clergymen. Keep this in mind.

Assessing the relevant parliamentary legislation

In the wake of Wolsey's downfall, parliament aimed to further reduce clerical abuses (and prove that they could). Three new Acts set limits on clerical fees and regularised mortuary and burial dues, combated pluralism and non-residence and other 'extra-curricular' employments. This last Act included a clause against further papal dispensations. Exemptions would now be purchased from the crown. In effect, this neatly curtailed papal authority and advanced royal power and, moreover, limited the monies Rome received from England and reduced the clergy's customary autonomy from lay authority.

Assessing the attack on other churchmen

None of this forced the Pope to resolve the divorce issue, but Henry had other options. One was an appeal to the old, rather vague, acts of *praemunire* (of 1353 and 1393) that forbid suits being prosecuted in foreign courts if they could otherwise be solved domestically. Broaden the meaning enough, and any Englishman working for a foreign power could be tried for treason.

On 11 July 1530, *praemunire* suits were filed in King's Bench (from which there was no appeal) against fourteen clerics (including eight bishops) on the grounds that they had aided and abetted Wolsey's legatine authority – they had all worked for Rome! The details of their relationships with Wolsey, or why these particular men were singled out, are unimportant; it was mere subterfuge anyway. What matters for us is that Henry had successfully executed a plan to scare every clergyman in the country. The penalty for *praemunire* could be death.

> *You are there ...*
> If you were a priest, with Wolsey as highest clerical and temporal authority, was there any way you could have avoided obeying his authority (and thus abetting it)? Indeed, how could you perform any of your duties without recognising Rome's authority? And, as such dignitaries as bishops could be charged with treason, who would save you? The Pope?

Had this solved the divorce issue?

No, but Henry gained two advantages.

1. The Pope would see parliament (the political nation) supporting their king and succeeding in curtailing papal authority.

2. The English clergy would see that the Pope could not protect them should Henry turn his anger against them.

Disagree or dispute royal authority at your peril! The obvious next step was to test how far crown authority could go.

The 'supreme headship'

In essence, Henry and his advisors were still trying to find a means of legitimately resolving the divorce issue without foreign intervention. They explored two related options:

1. Further limiting papal authority.
2. Expanding royal authority.

Understanding how papal authority could be limited

Recall that parliament had already, albeit in a limited way, restricted clerical power. Could it do more?

When Henry had allowed parliament to enact anti-clerical legislation there had been an up-roar in convocation. Never before had laymen interfered in strictly clerical matters. But there had been many other grievances voiced in the House of Commons which were not acted upon at the time. To forestall further interference, the clergy attempted reforming themselves. Thus, when convocation met again in January 1531, the clergy debated ideas for over 20 statutory reforms, ranging from attire to heresy (the main subject). Of course, the clergy's already extensive heresy controls were themselves sore points with the laity and, it all came to naught anyway, when Henry made his own pre-emptive strike.

Understanding the 'submission of the clergy' and the 'supreme headship'

Previously, 14 clergymen had faced *praemunire* convictions. Now, Henry threatened all of them; so, potentially, all titles and possessions would be subject to confiscation. The clergy were given the option, via their convocations, to purchase pardons for their illegal activities. In return for £100,000 plus expenses from southern convocation (and a roughly equivalent value of £19,000 from northern convocation), Henry would pardon them. A codicil was added, however, which stated that Henry was 'sole protector and supreme head of the Church in England', implying he had clerical powers of his own. You might find it odd that a layman would claim spiritual authority, but the clergy took little note of it, bothered more by the payment schedule. Henry wanted the entire sum payable on demand. Warham tried to negotiate a few guarantees:

▶ for the church's ancient liberties and privileges
▶ for a comprehensive definition of *praemunire*
▶ for certain modifications to earlier parliamentary legislation.

This was a political miscalculation. Indeed, Henry gave Warham a list of further conditions they would have to meet to gain his royal pardon. What he would do, however, was:

▶ pledge peaceful conditions under which the church might attend to the 'cure of souls committed to his majesty'
▶ allow a full five years for payment
▶ confirm such privileges as did not offend his regality
▶ pardon the clergy for all past offences.

Even now, the clergy hesitated. Why?

You are there ...

You are a priest. Ask yourself, what does all this mean? What does 'offend his regality' mean? Did the new title mean more than Henry admitted? Where is £100,000, a large sum of money, to be found? What would your share be? Yes, past offences would be pardoned, but without a clear definition, how could future offences be avoided?

John Fisher, a well-respected bishop, spoke out vehemently against the new title and the other demands, and his opinion swayed many. To overcome the ill ease felt by some, Henry agreed that his new title could be augmented with the words '... after God', later amended to '... as far as the word of God allows', and he dropped claims to spiritual powers. The clergy accepted these conditions and the pardon was granted.

Did this solve the divorce issue?

No, but it was never meant to. What was established was that the clergy were bound to obey the crown. Henry remained loyal to the Catholic faith, said he would not interfere with the clergy's work, but still hoped to pressure the Pope on the divorce. Convocation was now in his royal pocket.

Understanding the wider use of parliamentary legislation

With his domination of the English clergy complete, Henry could focus pressure directly on the Pope through parliament (with Thomas Cromwell's advice). Thus, between 1532 and 1534, a series of Acts whittled away papal authority, while leaving the door open to rapprochement (up to 1534). They attacked the Pope's financial and jurisdictional position with the:

▶ Act in Conditional Restraint of Annates, 1532.
▶ Act in Restraint of Appeals, 1533.
▶ Act for the Submission of the Clergy, 1534.
▶ Act in Absolute Restraint of Annates, 1534.
▶ The Dispensations Act, 1534.
▶ Act annexing First Fruits and Tenths to the Crown, 1534.
▶ Act of Supremacy, 1534.
▶ Act Against the Papal Authority, 1536.

We need not examine the details here, but you should familiarise yourself with these acts (see Elton, G.R., *The Tudor Constitution*, 2nd edn., Cambridge, 1982).

Parliament was used to apply financial pressure by cutting off resources, beginning with annates – papal dues extracted from newly beneficed incumbents to spiritual livings – amounting to roughly £6,000 a year. But, what if the Pope retaliated by, say, withholding necessary documents? The Act also covered this eventuality. Should he withhold the documents, domestic provisions would come into force (that is, royal authority). When it later became clear that the Pope would make no concessions, the Act was put into practice by letters patent (9 July 1533) and confirmed by parliament in 1534. Royal nominees to senior clerical positions could not be blocked. When the clergy grumbled, the Commons accused them of 'disloyalty'.

A Common's committee presented the so-called 'supplication against the ordinaries' on 18 March 1532. This was a list of grievances that attacked, especially, convocation's autonomous legislative authority, along with delays in clerical courts, the number of holy days, prejudicial heresy trials, etc. Henry, famously, took no action save to pass the paper over to convocation for a reply. Stephen Gardiner, bishop of Winchester and a brilliant lawyer, took charge and claimed that clerical legislative authority was guaranteed by God's law – which no man could dispense. Sound familiar? Imagine how angry Henry must have been when his own words were used against him. On 27 April, he handed the reply back to the Commons' committee, inviting further scrutiny. The result is that the clergy:

▶ could no longer assemble without royal writ
▶ could no longer enact or execute new canons without royal assent
▶ were required to submit all previous canons to a mixed lay/clerical
   commission for re-examination.

Henry then examined the bishops' consecration oaths, finding them '... but half our subjects, yea, and scarce our subjects' (Wilkins, iii.754). On 16 May, Warham presented an abject submission, itself later enacted (1534). As yet, however, Henry was no closer to a divorce, but the groundwork was complete. It was time for a direct assault.

Understanding the expansion of royal authority

One option was via parliament, of course; so successful against the Pope. But, Henry had to be seen as religiously orthodox; he could not leave himself open to questions of morality or heresy. Could royal authority be expanded without appearing to do anything innovative? Yes, if it could be shown that the papacy had usurped royal authority in the past. The way forward was either:

▶ find precedents for English autonomy from papal authority, or,
▶ uncover a means to surmount papal authority altogether.

Assessing the search for precedents

In brief, this was a hopeless failure. Henry wanted proof of a so-called *privilegium Angliae* – proof that no case could be removed from English to papal courts without expressed royal agreement. Nominally, the *praemunire* statutes addressed this point, but where was it clearly stated? The divorce could be settled in England, if only this statement could be found. Those scholars already searching the continental universities (on divorce matters) were ordered to explore libraries and archives for useful corroborating material for the *privilegium Angliae*. They found nothing; the *privilegium* was a myth.

Assessing the methods of surmounting papal authority

To a certain extent, parliament showed the way, but Henry was cautious and explored all options. Remember that question of 'legitimacy'? There were two possible approaches to this problem.

1.   Further explorations of royal authority.
2.   Further development of anti-papal theories.

Point one is merely an expanded effort into initiatives we have already examined, so let us concentrate on point two.

Understanding the anti-papal approach

If nothing else, it could be shown that the papacy had, over the years, usurped authority from the church (as a corporate body). For instance, Henry's scholars found that the canons of the Council of Nicea (325 AD) had concluded that no spiritual case should be taken out of the ecclesiastical province in which it originated. Thus, enshrined in history was the principle of local judicial autonomy. Could this find be exploited? Henry suggested that:

▶ the Bishop of London and Gregory Casali (an Italian agent) be elevated to cardinalships for a third *ex officio* papal 'divorce' trial in England;

▶ the case be committed to three English abbots (Kidderminster, Islip and Capon);

▶ the Bishop of London (as Henry's ordinary) should oversee a new trial alone;

▶ a third *ex officio* trial be summoned to a neutral location (Calais or Guisnes), with judges selected by Henry, Catherine (or Charles V), the Pope and Francis I (*Calender of State Papers (CSP)*), vii/v.310).

Neither the theories of papal infallibility nor papal indefectibility yet existed (the Pope could err and was corruptible). Henry did not have these obstacles, but the Pope could still, and did, reject Henry's pleas for 'justice'. Could Henry go over the Pope's head to a general council?

Understanding conciliarism

This is a pseudo-democratic theory that gives general councils (representing the entire church) higher authority than popes. In theory, if the Pope continued to frustrate Henry's needs (or declare for Catherine), he could appeal to a general council. Research now turned in this direction; the scholars finally assembling enough materials for three famous documents – *Collectanea satis copiosa*, *Glasse of Truthe* and *Articles Devised by the holle consent of the Kynges moste honourable counsayle*. You would do well to familiarise yourself with these primary sources. The advantages of conciliarism seem obvious:

▶ papal authority could be circumvented by orthodox methods
▶ a council could be summoned anywhere to solve a problem.

As a cudgel to beat the Pope, conciliarism had potential, save for one small problem:

▶ it could be summoned by the Emperor and the Pope too.

In any case, as other initiatives were dropped and, as financial, legislative and judicial pressures failed, the threat of an appeal became more attractive (in the short term). Indeed, on 29 June 1533, Henry did appeal, before Archbishop Lee (of

York), against the pope to a future council as a precaution should he be excommunicated (*Letters and Papers of the reign of Henry VIII (LP)*, vi.721.) Further research uncovered more material, collected and collated, preached as sermons and published in polemics – all asserting the general council's superiority. The central message was that the 'Bishop of Rome' had no more authority in England than any other foreign bishop.

Understanding the value of conciliarist theory

Henry would never have an airtight argument. Neither theology nor canon law – based as they are on theory and opinion – offer absolutes; counter-arguments would always be available. But, he had a reasonable case against papal supremacy. In light of the Act of Supremacy, however, conciliarism was put aside. Having put a question mark over papal supremacy, though, royal authority could be legitimately emphasised.

Assessing the further expansion of royal authority

Re-examine the royal headship. What the scholars needed to do now was prove that it was nothing new; to show that Henry had not usurped papal authority, but rather had re-claimed lost royal authority. It was not a new idea because:

▶ the royal headship had been acknowledged;

▶ kingship as 'divine office' was the central theme of William Tyndale's *Obedience of a Christian Man* (which Henry had read);

▶ Henry VII had been declared 'a person with dual characteristics, having both lay and ecclesiastical authority' (see: Geoffrey de C. Parmiter, 'A note on some aspects of the Royal Supremacy of Henry VIII', *Recusant History* x (1969–70), pp. 183–92).

The question was just how much spiritual power Henry actually had.

A number of polemics were written on this issue, including, *Oratio, De vera differentia* and *De vera obedientia*. You should familiarise yourself with these primary sources but, in brief, these argued that, in the past, kings:

▶ Had reproved clerical morals.
▶ Were recognised as responsible for the salvation of their subjects' souls.
▶ Were recognised as God's vicars (answerable to God alone).
▶ Had repressed heresy and error.
▶ Had lent this power out to local clergymen.

Most significantly, such polemics underlined two important concepts. They hinted that Henry possessed *potestas ordinas* (true sacerdotal, sacramental spiritual power), and affirmed his *potestas jurisdictionis* (administrative and judicial powers over the church as a corporate body). Although this did not solve the divorce issue, it did remove the final obstacles.

Understanding how the divorce could now be resolved

All of these documents, polemics and arguments underlined Henry's claim to imperial authority over his domains, meaning he was answerable only to God. This was the principle enshrined in the introduction to the Act of Appeals (extended in 1534).

The Act banned appeals from England to Rome on cases involving marriage, wills, clerical dues and fines – removing the last vestiges of papal authority. Cases would be tried (as before) in clerical courts, but there would be no appeal, save to the Crown. Thus, the Archbishop of Canterbury, Thomas Cranmer, the metropolitan of the realm, would decide the issue. By this point, Henry and Anne were already married and she was pregnant. All that remained was to ensure the legitimacy of any new heirs.

Understanding the Acts of Succession and Treason

Unsurprisingly, many nobles and commoners alike questioned whether Henry had acted legitimately against Catherine. It became necessary, therefore, to put into statute form some kind of guarantee of obedience. The first Succession Act (1534) set out the succession as follows:

▶ Henry's male heirs by Anne
▶ male heirs of any subsequent wives
▶ the princess Elizabeth and her children
▶ any subsequent daughters.

Most significantly, an oath was prepared in support of these details; writing or acting in opposition was treason. To accept any male heirs by Anne as legitimate would mean accepting the entire process, from 1527 to 1534, as legitimate too.

The royal supremacy

This was merely the putting into statute form all of the clerical concessions made up to 1534. The new Act recognised Henry's authority over heresy and church administration, and his right to conduct visitations and amend spiritual jurisdiction. The church dare not oppose him nor, in reality, could it. There was opposition, however.

Assessing the opposition

A number of people opined that the king had simply usurped traditional authority for his own petty ends; to some, he had become a heretic and/or a tyrant. Despite treason charges and imprisonments, others always seemed willing to take up opposition, including:

- ▶ the nun or 'holy maid' of Kent
- ▶ the Observant Franciscans
- ▶ the Carthusians
- ▶ John Fisher (Bishop of Rochester)
- ▶ Thomas More.

Elizabeth Barton, the 'holy maid', was a minor visionary who had decried the divorce many times (even to Henry's face) but had been ignored. When the marriage was annulled in 1533, however, she predicted Henry's deposition (a treasonable offence). In April (1534) she, and some followers were executed. The Franciscans and Carthusians had all of their properties confiscated and some of their members were arrested. Executions followed, but these men became martyrs, and the monks' resolution was never broken. The same is true of John Fisher. Having been implicated in the Barton case, and having refused to swear the oath of succession (as it denied papal authority), he was sentenced to be imprisoned in the Tower of London in April 1534. There he may have stayed except his letters addressed to Charles V had been found, suggesting he 'crusade' against Henry (another treasonable offence).

The case of Thomas More is slightly different. You should familiarise yourself with More, as historians are at loggerheads over him – saint or fanatic, genius, fool, humanist, lawyer or scholar? Was he, as it seems, a genuine 'friend' of the king? He presents the ideal opportunity for you to flex your analytical muscles.

What is certain about More is that he was considered virtuous and, more importantly, he was known to be virtuous. He was also very clever, and resisted speaking out directly against Henry's initiatives until it no longer mattered. Historians think he opposed the divorce and the royal supremacy because he agreed with Fisher that the Pope was the legitimate vicar of Christ on Earth – he just never said so publicly, counting on the legal principle that 'silence' means 'consent'. More, however, always maintained that he would support Henry to the limits of his conscience – beyond which he would not 'oppose' him. To Henry, this was the worst of betrayals. In the end, More refused the oath, was convicted of treason, and was executed a month after Fisher.

TUTORIAL

Summary of key ideas

- ▶ **Papal bulls** – any papal edict, so called because the symbol of the Pope is a bull.

- ▶ **Decretal commission** – the Pope's permission from certain judges to sit in consideration of spiritual matters.

- ▶ **Affinity** – a bar to marriage between a man and his wife's relatives to the fourth degree based on the 'relationship' which developed between them due to marriage or sexual intercourse.

▶ **Consanguinity** – like **affinity** but based on the 'blood' relationship implied by the idea that the husband and wife became 'as one flesh' due to marriage.

▶ **Public honesty** – a legal impediment to marriage based on earlier 'contracts'.

▶ **Divine law** – God's law or natural law as decreed by God in the Bible.

▶ **Annulment** – a declaration that a marriage never took place.

▶ **Levirate** – an ancient Jewish custom regarding inheritance practices.

▶ **Simony** – the buying and selling of ecclesiastical privilege or office.

▶ **Nepotism** – unfair advantages given to relatives.

▶ **Non-residence** – the practice where a clergyman lives somewhere other than the seat of his spiritual office.

▶ **Pluralism** – the practice of holding more than one clerical office simultaneously.

▶ **Sexual incontinence** – a lack of self-restraint.

▶ **Attainder** – a treason charge initiating forfeiture of properties, offices and often resulting in execution.

Progress questions

1. Why did Henry VIII need a 'divorce'?

2. Why did Henry place so much emphasis on theology?

3. How did the Pope's refusal to grant a divorce lead ultimately to schism?

Discussion points

1. Did Henry have a sound argument against his first marriage?

2. Did Henry have a sound argument for assuming so much authority personally?

Practical assignment

You will probably encounter 'challenge-type' questions (like, 'Henry VIII had a legitimate basis for complaint against his marriage to Catherine of Aragon' – Do you agree or disagree, and why?). To prepare, make a chart of several columns, listing theological, canonistic, political and (perhaps even) moral arguments for and against the Aragon marriage to help you decide.

Study and revision tips

You might well be asked to write about the divorce or the royal supremacy in an essay or an exam. With this in mind, you should:

1. Create a chronological outline of the main events (c.1527–1533) with some commentary on the motivations of the main figures involved (Henry, Catherine, Wolsey, Anne, Charles V, Clement VII, etc.)

2. Create a thematic outline of the main events (c.1530–1534) with some commentary on how one event lead to another (e.g., how the downfall of Wolsey led to questions about papal and royal authority).

Henry VIII – Flirting with Lutheranism

One-minute summary – After 1534, Henry tried to remain spiritually orthodox and achieve his political ends but, pursuit of the latter necessitated a closer association with Lutherans (Protestants) and radical thinkers who advocated the elimination of 'papist' rites and ceremonies. Henry tried to find a compromise position because the church in England needed real spiritual reform and real independence from Rome, but it also needed to avoid heresy. This chapter will help you to understand:

▶ the term *via media*
▶ the key issues of doctrine and ceremony
▶ the key influences on Henry
▶ the *Valor Eccesliasticus* and the dissolution of the monasteries
▶ the various formularies of faith
▶ the extent of reform, c.1547.

The *via media*

Post-supremacy, radicals wanted Henry to pursue more revolutionary ends, seeing 'Lutheranism' as a useful model, but conservatives urged him to protect England from that self-same model. Ideally, stability could be ensured if a genuine middle ground could be found. The problem was that religious positions became entrenched and the split was wider than was immediately obvious.

Understanding the extent of 'disunity'
Within a relatively short time (about six years) the religious leadership of England had changed dramatically. What had once been an independent body was now a corps of royal ecclesiastical ministers beholden to Henry. Where once they thought, taught and acted in unison, advocating traditional values, they now expressed a wide variety of opinions at loggerheads with one another, spreading divisive opinions. The promotion and execution of a workable doctrinal settlement, however, was placed squarely on their shoulders (there was no help from Henry). Of course, their disunity spread throughout the ranks. Moreover, Henry and his spiritual advisors had different agendas too.

The bishops focused on:

▶ limiting extreme religious movements (e.g. Anabaptism)
▶ the appropriate degree of reform
▶ the preservation of their own Episcopal authority.

Henry wanted to balance the needs of international security with domestic stability.

The key doctrinal and ceremonial issues

Between 1534 and 1540, Henry tried to entice various German Lutheran princes into peace negotiations because:

► he needed a counter-balance to threats from Catholic France and the Holy Roman Empire
► he wanted additional support for divorce and supremacy issues
► he had no other options.

The problem was that the various princes (like John Frederick, duke of Saxony) wanted him to endorse the 'Augsburg Confession' (the Lutheran religious statement) in exchange. Orthodox Catholic that he was, Henry refused, but would consider a compromise. This was possible because the true difference between Catholicism and Lutheranism, while important, is slight, with three issues outstanding:

► justification theology
► the interpretation and use of the Bible and tradition
► the seven sacraments.

Understanding traditional 'justification' theology

What do you need to do to get into heaven? The answer is that you must be righteous or free of the taint of sin. But, all humans are tainted by the sins of Adam (pride and faithlessness).

Picturing the scene ...
You go to church and confess your sins and the priest absolves you. But, no matter how moral you are and, no matter how often you confess, you are still a sinner and still guilty. Even if you were a paragon of virtue, simply by having been born you are guilty of original sin by association.

Except for original sin, you could reduce your guilt by performing good works and acts of charity (including donations to the church). In theory, God gave 'fallen' man a chance – observe the Ten Commandments and live by the example of Jesus – and salvation could be partially earned. Lutherans rejected this in favour of *solafideism* or *justification by faith alone*. This meant that salvation resulted merely by believing in God's promise of grace through the sacrifice of Jesus. Thus, the guilt of sin was unconditionally washed away by God's free grant of grace; your soul was regenerated; you could begin anew to act in a morally virtuous manner (or be 'born-again'). However, Luther was not the supreme head of a vast ecclesiastical organisation – collecting tithes, dues, fees and renting out properties.

You are there ...

As a layman, you have often confessed to a priest, done penance, and performed good works so that some of your guilt would be removed. In Lutheran practice, you need only to believe: there is no need for priests or for good works or acts of charity and no need to give money to the church.

Can you imagine Henry VIII going through all the trouble of the last six years only to agree, for the sake of placating relatively weak allies, that he was the head of a meaningless organisation that should be dismantled?

Understanding the use and importance of the Bible and tradition

Scripture underscores Christianity, although Catholicism accorded it little real importance otherwise. Catholics viewed it as merely equal to man-made traditions. It is true that a few biblical passages were incorporated into the liturgy, but these were read in Latin (incomprehensible to most laymen, and some clergy too). Scripture seemed to be on a 'need to know' basis. There was, however, some movement toward having the Bible officially translated into English, but these projects rarely advanced because, although it was the central source of theology, there were problems with:

▶ the Bible, which was imprecise on many important matters
▶ some passages were obscure in meaning
▶ some passages contradicted others.

Therefore, wouldn't the average layman be more confused than enlightened by reading the Bible? Wouldn't he also be subject to inflammatory interpretations? Scholars and lawyers could only guess at what certain passages meant. Collected together over the years, their assumptions and guesses became traditional practices that, over time, became dogmas so that before the Reformation, scripture and collected tradition became equal sources of truth. Moreover, as scripture was silent on a number of issues, unwritten or oral traditions were also collected and given similar respect. Obviously, just about anything could be justified in this way. Luther rejected it all in favour of *sola scriptura* (scripture as the only source of truth). He claimed it was the only religious authority and only test of spiritual legitimacy (all else was mere opinion), and Luther wanted it to be available to everyone in their own language. He said that if difficult passages were read sincerely, the Holy Spirit and right reason would make the meaning plain to the 'true' believer – a nice, but flawed theory.

Understanding the seven sacraments

The seven sacraments are rites and ceremonies that have special spiritual qualities; they convey divine grace to the recipients through the intervention of the priest. The priest performs the ritual and works a miracle. Traditionally, there are seven sacraments (baptism, confirmation, Eucharist, extreme unction, matrimony, ordination and penance). Priests (and only priests) performed the rites and, usually, only in Latin (the liturgy), so that only priests fully understood them. The sacraments and, therefore, participation in the church, was something performed on behalf of the laity. Luther regarded this as an insult. There were also other problems. The sacraments:

▶ were less important to the early church fathers;
▶ were not based exclusively on scripture;
▶ had medieval additions or man-made traditions tacked on;
▶ bolstered the separation of priests and laymen.

Luther believed that priests stood between God and man and, after due consideration, he rejected four of them and questioned another. Luther's reasons were that:

▶ Logic dictated that everyone was equally a member of the community of the faithful, so what need was there for priests imposing themselves between God and believers?

▶ As all seven sacraments could not be proven exclusively by scripture, they could not all be divine.

How is this significant?

As ordination, for instance, is central to the Catholic hierarchy, it also underpinned the structure of the English church. However, as Luther could find no scriptural justification for it, he concluded that all people have the same priestly powers (*the priesthood of all believers*) and only through the consent of the entire community could certain people exercise those powers for the sake of all. If this was the case, would Henry still be supreme head of the church? What about his patronage power (and subsequent income)? Luther also objected to how penance had been used to enforce moral and law-abiding behaviour.

You are there ...

You live in a small, tight-knit community. A priest can withhold absolution, deny God's forgiveness and, even, excommunicate you from the church. How would you live without personal interaction? No one would talk to or trade with you, and you could not attend church services. What would you be willing to do to get back into the priest's (and hence God's) good graces? Should priests have this power?

Luther thought they shouldn't. Moreover, by denying penance he destabilised a well-established disciplinary system. Can you imagine Henry abolishing a key element of national stability? And, if all people were equally priests and could interpret scripture for themselves, what need was there for a supreme head doing it on their behalf? Consider the implications.

What about the Eucharist and baptism?

Both Protestant and Catholic religions recognise these as true sacraments; both are clearly justified in scripture. But, for Luther, any true believer was a vessel of divine power and could, therefore, perform a sacrament. He saw baptism as merely an introduction to the community of the faithful, not a sacrament conferring grace upon the recipient.

Luther's thinking on the Eucharist is similar, but more complex. He also assumed **real presence** in the wine and bread (as in Catholicism), but denied that grace was conferred through participation in the ceremony or that any miracle was performed. He also rejected the idea of withholding the wine from the laity, as merely another measure of separation between them and the clergy. By approving the giving of sacrament *in both kinds* to everyone, the idea that all believers were of equal worth was reinforced. Without a miracle, however, just how were the bread and wine changed? (This change is known as *transubstantiation*.)

Transubstantiation depends on the philosophical acceptance that there are two aspects to the reality of objects – mental and physical. The physical aspect or 'accident' is what we see or touch, while the mental aspect or 'essence' is that more intangible quality that everyone seems to understand.

Picturing the scene ...

Imagine a table. The 'accident' of a table is wood, but obviously not everything made of wood is a table. The 'essence' of the table (as we all know) differentiates it from a plank, a stool or a chair. The 'accidents' of all these items is wood; their 'essences' differentiate them.

Traditionally during the Mass it was the essence of the bread and the wine that were transformed by the priest into the flesh and blood of Jesus, the accidents remaining unchanged and clearly visible as bread and wine. Luther rejected this in favour of what historians call *consubstantiation* (meaning 'coexistence'), the philosophical possibility that more than one element could be present in any object at any time. Therefore, the bread remains bread (its essence unchanged) but the body of Jesus coexists with it in time and space. There is no 'miracle' of transformation; the *real presence* merely shares the space in some other mysterious way (which Luther never explained).

> *Picturing the scene ...*
> Imagine a blacksmith and an iron rod. The rod remains a rod even when it is heated in a fire to a white-hot state. The rod and the fire share the same space. The blacksmith did not put the fire into the rod, he was merely the instrument by which the rod was put into the fire.

Often, the tiniest differences of opinion can drive a wedge between people. Luther's theology, in many ways, offended both Henry and some of his chief ministers. Having now seen where important divisions between them lay, could you have found a compromise? Attempts were made but, ultimately, to little gain. First, let us examine a more practical expression of reform, the dissolution of the monasteries (on which all parties agreed).

The *Valor Ecclesiasticus*

Some church taxation, dues and fines had been transferred to Henry. Just how much were these worth? How much were individual offices worth? In theory, to reform the church, Henry needed to know just how big it was, so a full-scale inspection of the holdings and values was undertaken. The result was the *Valor Ecclesiasticus* (or ecclesiastical valuation), Thomas Cromwell's 1535 initiative.

Assessing the results
We need not go into great detail, but you should examine them some time. A few examples will suffice.

- ▶ The diocese of Winchester (the richest) had an annual income of c.£4,000.
- ▶ The diocese of London had an annual income of c.£1,100.
- ▶ The diocese of Bangor (the poorest) had an annual income of c.£150.

This was the kind of information Henry needed. Those figures meant he could expect c.£525 a year in payments, fines and dues. The valuation also showed that the church was badly administered, particularly the monasteries. But, did they really have to be dissolved?

Dissolution of the monasteries

Most historians doubt Henry's motives, believing that the dissolution was a purely money-making venture. There is little to suggest otherwise and, at the time, few people opposed it. But we should not dismiss the possibility that there were other (less compelling) reasons.

What were these other reasons?

Leaving aside the obvious financial one, other reasons suggested include:

▶ the international situation
▶ the political power of abbots and priors
▶ theological consistency
▶ the regulars' social and cultural powers
▶ obvious administrative and disciplinary problems.

It will be left for you to decide if these other reasons have any validity, but let us briefly consider a few.

Abbots, priors and the international situation

Recall the Acts of Appeals and Supremacy, through which the English church had been insulated from all outside influences. The knock-on effect was that Henry, and England, were isolated from continental political alliances and were viewed with suspicion (and envy), and, in some quarters, charged with heresy. The idea that members of a religious order (in England) owed allegiance to a parent institution (outside England) was anachronistic and politically dangerous. Were monasteries hotbeds of resistance? Probably not, but there were some trouble spots (e.g., the Carthusians – see page 24). Plead loyalty and accept reforms though they might, Henry could not risk any potential threats.

Keep in mind that there were some 27 or so abbots and priors who had the right, due to their temporal power and official wealth, to attend parliament. You may have heard the term 'lords-spiritual' before (it is still in use). It refers to these men, and bishops, sitting in the House of Lords. They also sat in both houses of convocation. Now, convocation may have been in decline, but parliament was still an important institution, and the Lords particularly so. If you were Henry, would you assume that the abbots and priors would continue to support your reforms?

'Theological consistency'?

This questions the purpose of a monastery and monastic life. In essence, monasteries are 'purgatorial institutions'.

Remember that the question of purgatory had been brought into doubt. Consequently, were institutions that offered up prayers and masses for their founders and benefactors (and their families) to limit their time in purgatory still necessary? Chantry priests could say these prayers instead. Monasticism was not itself a fundamental part of Catholic doctrine. Monastic functions – devotion to worship, celebration of the Mass, performance of good works and acts of charity – were all in doubt. Therefore, the dissolution could be presented as a vital step in revitalising the spiritual life of the nation.

What about their obvious social and cultural roles?

In brief, some 10% of England's wealth was in monastic hands and individual houses were often the single largest employers (of estate or farm workers) in any given area. They also provided schools and hospitals and, more often than not, a community's only religious centre. They provided everything from counselling to the settlement of various disputes. Indeed, some houses were centuries old, and key to local history, tradition and pride. There were clear arguments to be made for sparing certain houses if, for example, they provided a locality's only school. But, influential as they were over the lay world, a great problem was the increasing influence of the lay world over them. There were obvious administrative and disciplinary problems.

In general, though, historians maintain it was not really all that bad. Most monks were devoted, studious and humble and most monasteries fulfilled their duties with all due concern and piety. Like anti-clericalism, however, there were some spectacular failures tainting the entire institution, which for example:

▶ encouraged an immoderate veneration of images and relics;
▶ did not have the requisite number of inmates or were heavily in debt; and
▶ allowed civilian clothing and fashions.

Some abbots and priors treated the monastery's property as their own or even chose to live elsewhere. In other cases, sexual incontinence and perversion was observed while, in others, heresy had been detected. Some buildings were dilapidated, some monks:

▶ did not read the Bible at regular times or converse in Latin
▶ were charged with criminal offences!

But, most damning, however, was the fact that every year, fewer and fewer people were adopting the monastic life – there seemed less and less value attributed to it.

Obviously, we have to be careful not to paint all monks, friars and nuns with the same brush. As is true today, the expression 'no news is good news' was applicable. If a monastery exhibited no problems, then no one would hear about it – they would only know about the problems. But a general feeling of apathy towards monasticism was apparent among the laity. The regulars were not hated, but nor were they loved, but they were taken for granted. In any case and, for whatever reasons, monasteries were dissolved. How was this achieved?

The method of dissolution

Monastic dissolution was an old idea. Monasteries had been amalgamated or dissolved in the past and their wealth put to other uses (like founding colleges). Wolsey, with Cromwell's assistance, had founded schools at Oxford and Ipswich in this way. The procedure of dissolution was simple.

▶ There was a visitation by a superior (a provincial or diocesan ordinary).

▶ This led to recommendations for improvement (or dissolution).

▶ If improvements were not made the monastery was dissolved, its members moved elsewhere and any revenues re-allocated.

So, when in January 1535 Cromwell became Henry's vicegerent in spirituals, he organised a visitation from which a valuation was calculated. What was different from previous visitations was the number of laymen involved, men who were on the lookout for specific problems (which, of course, they found). A distressing picture was assembled which Cromwell took to parliament for resolution to ask what could be done. (Of course, he already had a plan, the Dissolution of the Monasteries Act of 1536.)

All houses with an annual income below £200 (approximately 300 monasteries and most nunneries) were dissolved and their wealth passed into crown possession. You should note, however, that monks and nuns were given the option of either moving to other establishments or opting out of the religious life altogether (some with hefty pensions!). Whether the dissolutions would have stopped at the lesser houses is a debatable issue. Some historians think this was a 'one-off' operation to secure immediate funds, while others claim that Cromwell planned to eventually dissolve them all. Fearing further dissolutions, some abbots abandoned their brethren to save themselves (hoarding or hiding treasure for their own future use). In this way, the heart went out of English monasticism save for a token opposition (see below). The second Act of Dissolution (1539) dissolved the remaining monasteries, friaries and nunneries, but gave some of the inmates pensions or, where applicable, benefices.

Assessing the reasons for the dissolutions

Obviously, you must decide for yourself about Henry's sincerity and whether the dissolutions were necessary. Eight monastic cathedrals had been refounded as secular ones (with deans and chapters) – Norwich, Canterbury, Carlisle, Durham, Ely, Rochester, Winchester and Worcester – while six houses were refounded as cathedrals – Bristol, Chester, Gloucester, Oxford, Peterborough and Westminster. Two others became secular colleges. There was a plan for the development of new dioceses too, but having held back a substantial proportion of monastic wealth, some new foundations were economically unviable.

The consequences of dissolution

Besides approximately 8,000–9000 regulars being forced to find other occupations, there were very real and severe results, particularly in the surrounding lay communities.

Assessing the aftermath in social, economic and cultural terms

For the crown, the dissolution was a great financial success. It allowed Henry to fund wars against France and Scotland later. Moreover, the gentry and nobles were able to acquire good lands at a reasonable market price (selling at a profit later), as well as new status symbols, like plates and statuary. Moreover, they acquired a greater voice in church patronage. That is to say, they now had a more decisive voice in the church of the future, as they now nominated and appointed its local officers. But, what about the physical loss?

▶ Examples of mediaeval architecture were destroyed as the buildings were plundered for materials (and the remainder left to decay).

▶ Mediaeval art works were sold off and lost to posterity.

▶ Gold and silver were melted down.

▶ Lead was used for other purposes.

▶ The poor were left without their sources of charity.

The impact of this is difficult to assess. You will have to decide for yourself, for example, the importance of the loss of one example of mediaeval architecture or whether the loss of one source of charity was really significant (given the vastness of the problem of the poor as a whole). This is not to suggest that no one cared, after all, there was opposition; you have to be careful not to read only one side of the argument.

Assessing the opposition

That there was opposition suggests that people were not as apathetic as we might suppose. The difficulty facing us is that there was not a lot of opposition and, what there was, was ineffectual and self-serving. Those who had never shown a genuine devotion to monasticism before could not credibly do so now. The Pilgrimage of Grace, sometimes mistakenly viewed as an uprising against the dissolutions *in toto*, was opposed only to the extent that it further burdened the northern economy. The leaders of the revolt argued that dissolution would only enrich southerners at the expense of northerners (noble northern families in particular). In this way, they hoped to enlist the help of the local landed gentry. Otherwise:

▶ Where would they deposit unmarried daughters and sisters, if not in nunneries?
▶ Where would they deposit aged relatives, if not in monasteries?
▶ How would they provide for third or fourth sons?
▶ Would they take on the burden of charity?
▶ Would they employ all the old monastic servants and keep the farms together?

Ultimately, these arguments failed. Why?

Henry was doing nothing illegal (if not morally suspect). As supreme head of the church he had no authority to answer to but his own (and God's). He was legally entitled to deal with the monasteries as he saw fit. The members were paid off, pensioned, given lump sums or beneficed, so there was little opposition from them. (Tudor society, in general, was a law-abiding one.) It is estimated that all but about 1,500 disposed regulars found some new life and, those who did not were mostly women who could, perhaps, be absorbed back into their families. Physical reforms were achievable. Why did religious authorities have so much trouble with doctrinal reform?

The formularies of faith

Henry, as a traditionalist and realist, would not pursue radical reforms because this would give his Catholic enemies (at home and abroad) an excuse for violence. Dissolving monasteries offended few people; advocating radical theology, however, was another matter. If Henry stressed tradition too firmly, he risked alienating the only potential continental allies remaining and, perhaps, lending tacit support to any reactionary backlashes. As a conscientious supreme head, Henry knew that reform was needed but, as a theological dilettante, he did not know how best to achieve it, turning the responsibility over to his religious advisors and bishops. Hardly unified themselves, it is not surprising that seven years of effort produced very little progress. But, with a widespread fear of violence, and the ever-increasing threat from radical sectarians, they had to try.

Assessing *The Ten Articles* (1536)
The convocation of 1536 is a watershed in English religious history for two reasons:

1.   It was the first official consideration of the *Wittenburg Articles*.

2.   The presentation of the *dogmata mala* (listing some 59 heretical opinions current in the realm) scared many.

Henry ordered convocation to initiate investigations into the essential questions of faith with the object of producing an official statement. With factional strife dogging them at every turn, the result was the *Ten Articles*, a statement that was a patchwork of Lutheran assertions which were modified and qualified by strict Catholic interpretations. It was vague on many issues, silent on others and, ultimately, designed to cause no offence.

Was there compromise on the disputed issues?
Not really. For instance, real presence in the Eucharist was agreed, but all other speculations were avoided. It accepted the importance of tradition (in written or

unwritten forms), avoided *solafideism*, and defended good works as vaguely useful. The only essentially non-Catholic statements were questions about purgatory and the cult of saints, meeting the Lutherans halfway. It dealt with only three sacraments (penance, baptism and the Eucharist) but did not explicitly reject the other four.

Was it ever officially used?
Yes, but only after a fashion. *The Ten Articles* was published under the guidance of Bishop Edward Fox and offered to convocation on 11 June 1536. Although many clergymen signed it, few were pleased. Indeed, royal injunctions were needed to enforce its use at the parochial level. If Henry thought that this would be the end of doctrinal division, however, he was sorely mistaken. A number of events forced him to reconsider.

▶ His isolation in Europe was eased as a war had broken out between Valois France and the Habsburgs (throughout most of 1536–37).

▶ Internal tension was heightened by the Pilgrimage of Grace and by the announcement of a plan to summon a general council at Mantua.

▶ The German princes pestered Henry for further negotiations.

▶ The *Ten Articles* had solved nothing.

As a result, the prelates were ordered to try again.

Assessing The Bishops' Book (1537)
The bishops and 25 or so junior clerics were summoned to meet in a synod (under Cromwell) to re-address those issues most in dispute with the Lutherans. The bishops, however, had their own agendas and rapidly split off into committees (along religious lines), thus impairing a project which already had too many objectives and diplomatic hopes pinned on it.

Was there compromise on the disputed issues?
There were slightly more than there had been in *The Ten Articles*.

▶ All seven sacraments were recognised, but unevenly weighted.

▶ Transubstantiation was glossed over again.

▶ Old traditions were accepted, but weighted below scripture (although neither *sola scriptura* nor *solafideism* were accepted outright).

▶ A clearer condemnation of image and saint veneration is evident.

The bishops all agreed on their right (subject to the supreme head) to make and ordain canons (no *priesthood of all believers* nonsense here).

Was this ever officially used?
Yes, but only after a fashion. Henry was unimpressed and gave it short shrift. Later, he made 246 changes. Moreover, it was far too long to ever be popular and was never ratified by convocation, parliament or the king. Eventually, it was published, sponsored only by the signatory bishops and theologians. Despite two failed attempts, a number of events conspired to force Henry to try again.

▶ New negotiations with the German princes had begun despite Henry's waning interests.

▶ The council of Mantua loomed closer.

▶ The Pope was about to publish a bull of excommunication against Henry.

▶ Some Anabaptists had been found in England.

▶ Henry, concerned with his international position, was considering Cromwell's idea of a foreign bride.

▶ By 1539, Charles V and Francis I were at peace (meaning they could concentrate their combined efforts on England).

Particularly because of the last, Henry had now to prove himself staunchly orthodox.

Assessing the Act of Six Articles (1539)
Where convocation had failed, perhaps the Lords could produce something useful. What emerged, however, was yet another vice-gerential synod (chaired by Cromwell), featuring a precise division of conservative and radical bishops. Moreover, it is a widely held opinion that Henry had already concluded on the matter and was only going through the motions. However, you should familiarise yourself with the Act.

Was there compromise on the disputed issues now?
No, compromise was not the aim. The conservatives had an in-built majority in the Lords and Henry's frequent participation reinforced their position. In brief, the Act was divided into six articles, each removing one radical interpretation.

▶ The first restated the Catholic understanding of the Eucharist and related dogma.

▶ The second discontinued communion *in both kinds*.

▶ The third rejected clerical marriage.

▶ The fourth addressed other marriage related issues (like widowhood).

▶ The fifth recognised private masses as 'meet and necessary'.

▶ The sixth found auricular confessions to be 'expedient and necessary'.

Clearly, *justification by faith alone* was ruled out. Moreover, a codicil featured harsh enforcement provisions and serious penalties, like burnings for heretics.

What was the result?
Almost immediately some 500 people were presented to the Bishop of London on heresy charges (some were burned) and measures against the reading of the Bible in English were proclaimed (people who possessed a copy were rounded up). These were short-term reactions, however, and by the end of the year Henry was once again in talks with the Lutherans. By April 1540, he appealed to the bishops once again.

Assessing *The King's Book* (1543)
The religious disunity of the senior clergymen was an insurmountable obstacle. But, Henry appointed another two committees – a group of bishops and theologians to examine doctrine and another group of bishops to assess the need for liturgical ceremonies. Now, even the timing was against them.

▶ They witnessed the fall of Cromwell.

▶ They witnessed the dissolution of the Cleves marriage and the new Howard marriage (both necessitating all new committees).

▶ They witnessed the Gardiner-Barnes-Cranmer public doctrinal disputes.

While we will not examine these other issues here, you should read about them. Ultimately, the work was of little impact and, when the time came, another committee merely recopied *The Bishops' Book*, incorporating Henry's several amendments, and presented it to convocation in April 1543.

Was there compromise on disputed issues?
Not really. Over the last 12 years, most of the senior clergymen had become so-called 'Henricians' – religious moderates who followed Henry's lead. Thus, the new formulary was, like the king, conservative on the major issues. If it could be called compromise, the section on prayers for souls departed finally dropped all references to purgatory (which at least reflecting Lutheran thinking).

What was the result?
Not much of a 'reformation' at all really. The ideological battle was political, no longer religious at all. In light of the royal supremacy and dampening down of clerical authority, progressive thinkers had entrenched themselves into positions at court, rather than in the church. More than anything else, this explains two things.
1.   The relative loss of interest in religious issues between 1543 and 1547.

2.   The immediate lurch to radical reform in the next reign.

TUTORIAL

Summary of key ideas
▶ **Solafideism** (*justification by faith alone*) – justification depends merely upon belief in the Grace of God.

▶ **Baptism** – the rite of initiation into the Church wherein a child was dipped into blessed water (to signify the death of Jesus) and then lifted out (to signify resurrection).

▶ **Confirmation** – the rite of ratification of baptism.

▶ **(The) Eucharist** – the rite in which the priest offers the dedication, transforms the bread and wine into the body and blood of Jesus (*transubstantiation*) which, in essence, caused Jesus to suffer death once again for the benefit (grace) of the recipients.

▶ **Extreme unction** – the last rite wherein the priest anoints the dying or terminally ill with unction (thereby granting grace).

▶ **Matrimony** – an odd rite wherein the priest merely performs the ceremony while the couple enter into the state of grace for themselves.

▶ **Ordination** – the rite by which a man becomes a priest through episcopal laying on of hands (which confirmed apostolic succession and conferred a special grace which could never be removed or lost)

▶ **Penance** – the rite by which the individual repented the shame of his sins, composed of five elements — contrition (shame), confession (admission of sin), satisfaction (performing a chore to earn forgiveness), regeneration (change of life), and absolution (the removal of the taint of sin by a priest).

▶ **Priesthood of all believers** – the belief that all believers are equal in the eyes of God and just as capable of spiritual leadership.

▶ **Real presence** – the belief that the blood and body of Christ is presence in the wine and bread of the Eucharist.

▶ **In both kinds** – the practice of giving both wine and bread to the laity during the Eucharist.

▶ **Transubstantiation** – the Catholic description of how the bread and wine change into the body and blood (the accidents remaining).

▶ **Consubstantiation** – the Lutheran description of how the bread and wine change into the body and blood (a sharing of the same space).

Progress questions

1. Why did Henry's change of status to 'supreme head' necessitate dissolving the monasteries?

2. What was the cause of disunity among the bishops and senior theological advisors?

3. What were the social, economic and cultural changes brought about by the dissolution of the monasteries, if any?

Discussion points

1. Why could Henry dissolve the monasteries but not successfully bring about an English translation of the Bible?

2. What prevented Henry from pursuance of Lutheranism in full?

3. Why did the formularies of faith fail to achieve what Henry wanted them to achieve?

Practical assignment(s)

1. Imagine yourself living at the time as a Catholic priest. Write a letter to the king advising him:
   a) why he should proceed with religious reform
   b) how this would best be achieved.

2. Imagine you are an important layman. Write a letter to a continental relative explaining how the dissolution of the monasteries is a good thing.

Study and revision tips

You might well be asked whether you think the reign of Henry VIII provided any real examples of reformation. To prepare, create a simple chart of two columns, headed 'traditional views and beliefs' and 'radical or Lutheran views and beliefs' and list all the instances you can think of in the appropriate column. This should help you visualise the events (e.g., sacrament in both kinds of religion is a radical view).

Edward VI – Protestant Restructuring

One-minute summary – Edward VI was a minor, which meant that he had to rely on leading adult politicians to set the government's agenda and advise him on all decisions (including religious ones). Having been educated as a Protestant and, surrounded by Protestant advisors, a reform movement in the direction of continental models was imminent. Direction, however, depended upon the regents – Edward Seymour and, later, John Dudley. Seymour pursued a moderate 'Lutheran' agenda, while Dudley looked toward the more radical 'Calvinist' model. Ultimately, they achieved little. This chapter will help you to understand:

▶ the influence of the regents
▶ the influence of Cranmer
▶ how key religious issues were resolved
▶ the role of parliament
▶ popular discontent
▶ the role of Lady Jane Grey
▶ the importance of the reign.

The influence of Edward Seymour

Edward's first regent was the Duke of Somerset. He was the king's uncle and took the grandiose title 'Lord Protector of the Realm and Governor of the King's Person' through letters patent on 12 March 1547. His position gave him nearly unlimited power over all aspects of government, sometimes without the royal council. This included a far-reaching religious authority. Like Henry VIII, however, he had no theological expertise, but his mild Protestant leanings directed him toward mild religious reforms (Lutheran in character). His main concern was military – he wanted to crush Scotland. To avoid domestic complications, he tried not to unduly upset Catholics (meaning Charles V in particular). Seymour can be easily summed up:

▶ as almost exclusively focused on Scotland (wanting to assert English claims on the Scottish throne through either a marriage or warfare)

▶ as tolerant of religious opinions not his own

▶ as committed to domestic order.

His preoccupations did create religious tension, however, as both populace and church now needed a strong central authority figure, which neither he nor Edward could provide.

How did the religious reform proceed?

'Piecemeal' sums it up. In essence, for both Seymour and the ruling élites, other matters simply came first. Moreover:

▶ the council was dominated by humanists with largely secular interests

▶ ecclesiastical commissions, dominated by lawyers, sought *via media* before radical reform

▶ the parochial clergy were largely conservative, less educated and less cosmopolitan than their superiors

▶ the bishops were still divided on many issues

▶ radical Protestant exiles returning to England tried the patience of their conservative brethren.

Given all this, that Seymour achieved anything is impressive. He proceeded, on the advice of Cranmer, using proclamations and statutes (as Henry VIII often had).

The influence of Thomas Cranmer (under Seymour)

If reformation was to proceed, a careful path had to be laid. Interested parties were faced with a mountainous task. An imperfect church, an ill-translated scripture, questionable interpretations of the sacraments, too much reverence paid to statues and images, relics, acts of charity, too little regard for God's pure saving Grace. Although Seymour favoured reform, he was unclear on how to direct it and the burden fell to Cranmer:

▶ as Archbishop of Canterbury
▶ as neither corruptible politician nor canon lawyer, but as a learned theologian whose priorities were spiritual
▶ as a married man with a stake in further reform
▶ as a scholar capable of changing his own mind and learning from the past.

Moderate religious reforms

What reforms were achieved? For the first few years (given the preoccupation with Scotland) the answer is significantly few. For instance, the injunctions of 1547 ordered:

▶ the removal of offensive or 'abused' statuary, relics, images and superstitious practices

▶ a visitation of all dioceses (providing a snapshot of conditions)

▶ that all parishes purchase a copy of Cranmer's *Book of Homilies* (which included Lutheran understandings of justification – *by faith alone* – and use of scripture, etc.)

▶ that all parishes purchase Erasmus' *Paraphrases*, an English Bible and copies of other important Protestant texts

▶ that services be conducted weekly and in English

▶ communion in both kinds of religion

▶ that the Henrician treason, heresy and censorship laws were unenforced.

This last point seems rather liberating. In theory, it allowed people to voice their opinions without fear of censure. Unfortunately, it also occasioned much violence and religious intolerance because:

▶ it encouraged religious debates, disputes and seditious preaching
▶ it initiated pamphlet wars on many difficult issues.

Indeed, as a result some 160 books by Protestant reformers were published. These encouraged the spread of extreme opinions, widespread iconoclastic vandalism, riots and violence against minority religious groups. Obviously, any image or opinion could offend someone.

You are there ...
Imagine yourself as an opinionated radical Protestant returned from exile. The new régime seems to be allowing you free reign to vent your spleen. Would you take up the option with gusto and try to save a few souls, or sit idly by to see what happens next? If someone spoke out against your opinions, would you defend them? How vigorously? Souls are at stake!

Understanding the role of parliament in the Seymour era

Given such problems, you might expect parliament to have been used as a healing salve for the nation's ills but, sadly, you would be wrong. Seymour used it merely to rubber-stamp what had already been done (and for his own desired ends against the Scots).

What was done?

With regard to religion, the 1547 session produced:

▶ The Chantries Act (which dissolved 2,374 chantries/chapels, 90 collegiate churches and 110 hospitals) in order to raise a war chest (and found some schools).

▶ A new Treason Act which increased freedom of expression (but left the authorities free to focus on war).

▶ A revocation of the Act of Six Articles, *The King's Book* and the Act for the Advancement of True Religion.

▶ Agreement that bishops would be appointed by letters patent thereafter (eliminating tedious and costly election processes).

You should familiarise yourself with these points in more detail. Sadly, none of this eased the tensions brought about by Seymour's social liberalism. New parliamentary legislation (September 1547) therefore, prohibited all public preaching. In theory, tensions would relax and Seymour could focus exclusively on war and, to a certain extent, this worked. By the third session (November 1548), tensions across the country had relaxed. Moreover:

▶ A successful invasion had significantly reduced the Scottish threat.

▶ Bishop Edmund Bonner had been deprived of London.

▶ Bishop Stephen Gardiner had been imprisoned (removed from the political scene).

▶ Bishops Veysey, Day and Heath had all resigned (allowing Protestants to take their places).

Religious questions could now be re-examined in a more proactive and positive way. This resulted in an Order of Communion (March 1548) and the first Edwardian Act of Uniformity (January 1549).

Did these represent real reform?

Yes, but not a revolution. This legislation was based on, and encouraged the use of, Cranmer's (First) *Book of Common Prayer* (one of the most important religious texts ever produced in England). It is important because:

▶ It gave the church an order of worship (drawn from a number of sources), a clear doctrinal definition and a regular and cyclic order of service.

▶ No penalties were laid out for lay non-attendance (enforcement was left to the bishops and clergy, who were also to test the knowledge of the parishioners).

▶ 'Common prayer' suggested a 'priesthood of all believers'.

▶ Its ambiguous statement on the Eucharist allowed for both Catholic or Protestant interpretation.

It is important to note, however, that the church remained ceremonially traditional in that:

▶ Clerical vestments and ritual regalia (candles, chrism of consecrated oil) were still used.

▶ A railed-off altar remained at the east end (rather than a communion table in the centre of the church – as was the practice in Geneva).

▶ Prayers for the dead, commemorations of the virgin and saints, confession and extreme unction were still in evidence.

To conservatives, these traditional remnants balanced such things as non-enforcement of clerical celibacy. This practise had been curtailed by parliament, giving married priests a vested interest in reformation. Celibacy was declared 'more desirable', of course. Moreover, wall paintings and images were destroyed and a few rituals (like creeping to the cross) discontinued. Unsurprisingly, except in the most conservative areas, there was little opposition to these changes but for some, even this was too much.

Assessing popular discontent

If there was little opposition to religion reforms *per se*, there were at least religious overtones to the rebellions of the 1547–49 period. For example, in the so-called 'Western' – or 'Prayer Book' – rebellion (which broke out in Devon in June 1549), there were both religious and linguistic complaints (preferring traditional Latin, or even Cornish, to the imposition of English). The real problem was that, after the dissolution of the chantries and Seymour's liberal ideas, people were angry when the government did not pick up the slack in charity and welfare donations. Nor did those humanist and Protestant councillors address crises in:

▶ monetary confidence (debasement of coinage, inflation)
▶ industry (wool trade, sheep farming)
▶ enclosures
▶ rising population and underemployment.

Changes to the liturgy did not ease bad harvests and starvation in the countryside. And, while economic and social problems are beyond our remit here, there are religious overtones in Seymour's and his advisors' morally suspect responses.

They had at least paid lip service to the concept of a 'common good' and had made all the appropriate noises against so-called 'private gains' (greed). Ultimately, they merely raised taxes and passed a few economically dedicated statutes. Sadly, none of it worked and, in fact, merely polarised the gentry and noble classes against the régime itself. Thus, when between June and August 1549 much of the country rose in rebellion, Seymour was caught between sympathy for the rebel cause (e.g., non-confidence in the government's agricultural policy) and the usual Tudor fears of social disorder. The two serious rebellions – the Western and (the more serious) Kett's Rebellion (in Norfolk in July 1549) left him politically isolated and, by 14 October, deposed and imprisoned. John Dudley, Earl of Warwick, rose to prominence having put down the latter uprising.

The influence of John Dudley

As they say, nothing succeeds like success and Dudley succeeded. But the many debates centred on his character and attitudes have left him an ill-understood personality. He captured power in the wake of Kett's Rebellion by playing up:

► his military successes
► Seymour's political isolation and ultimate incompetence
► the divisions between radicals and conservatives on the Privy Council
► gentry and aristocratic fears for their own economic and social positions.

Historians think that he is more conservative than Seymour (in his political and social ideas) but more radical (in religion). Even if aspects of Dudley are poorly understood, there can be no doubt that he was a successful political administrator and consummate politician.

Was he religiously radical?
His abandonment of the 1549 religious compromise certainly indicates radical convictions. Clearly, he encouraged a movement towards the reformed religion of Geneva and replaced (as opportunity allowed) conservative bishops with radicals. G. R. Elton, however, made a good case when he described Dudley's reasons for doing so as politically motivated.

Were Dudley to have abandoned the Reformation in 1549, re-invigorated clerical orders and establishments may have demanded their lands and properties back, while conservative bishops and other high-ranking officials may have sought more legislative autonomy (*England under the Tudors*, p. 209). However, while he may have been a Catholic all along (witness his switch back to Rome on the accession of Mary), he projected radical sentiments and encouraged religious reformation in order to achieve success and stability in other areas more important to him. Remember, Edward himself was in favour of further reforms. Whatever the truth and, keeping Dudley's search for stability in mind, the key religious issues of the period are fairly obvious and familiar.

The key religious issues

In essence, the church needed:

▶ A widely acceptable order of worship and service.
▶ A workable (if not exactly precise) doctrinal definition.
▶ Pliable officials who would be obedient to the supreme head in all things.

These officials would concentrate on spiritual rather than political matters and keep the lid on local discontent. Moreover, once the movement toward Geneva was under way and (to a certain extent) successful, more would be demanded. And, as Calvinism is a magisterial reform movement (that is, it combines both civic and spiritual elements and recognises the power of the civil authorities in religious matters) Dudley was quite happy to steer reform into this self-serving (although not necessarily bad) direction. The resolution of these issues was based on familiar methods:

▶ coercion of the remaining conservative bishops
▶ an appeal to parliament
▶ a reassessment of church wealth
▶ a re-examination of the articles of faith.

How were the bishops coerced?

They were simply given no choice. For example, although already in the Tower, when Gardiner refused to support further doctrinal change, he was given a harsher sentence and deprived of his see (February 1551). His replacement was John Poynet who, as Bishop of Rochester, was renowned for his radical sentiments and close association with Cranmer. Bonner was also retried, given a harsher sentence and deprived. His replacement, Nicholas Ridley, was a strict diocesan reformer. Indeed, many southern dioceses eventually had reforming bishops:

▶ John Scory (1551) was appointed to Rochester and later (1552) to Chichester.

▶ Thomas Thirlby was translated from Westminster to Norwich (1550).

▶ John Hooper was appointed to Gloucester (1550) and, *in commendam*, to Worcester (1552).

▶ Miles Coverdale was appointed to Exeter (1551).

These were radical thinkers who, unlike their conservative predecessors, had little or no interest in politics. They were far more interested in spiritual reform and, basically, Dudley left them to it while he concentrated his efforts elsewhere. In this way, radical reforms were introduced.

For example, while Cranmer set about the revision of the Prayer Book, Ridley ordered the replacement of all London altars with communion tables. He was one of the first to introduce the new ordinal (revised in parliament along a more 'Lutheran' formula), eliminating many of the lesser clerical offices and encouraged preaching. Hooper, a man who seemed to live and breathe the Gospel (acting only with specific biblical guidance), rigorously visited his parishes and focused on widespread re-education. The remaining conservatives were left bereft of effective leadership. Of course, the power of the new bishops depended on their continued support of the supreme head (via Dudley). But, therein lay a problem. Edward was not a hearty individual and his obvious successor, Mary, was Catholic. Dudley thus turned to parliament for, hopefully, a solution.

The role of parliament (under Dudley)

Over the course of Dudley's régime as Lord President of the Council, parliament was in session on three occasions:

> 4 November to 1 February 1550
> 23 January to 15 April 1552
> 1–31 March 1553

and he made good use of them.

What was achieved?

On the first occasion, a new ordination procedure was developed along with a measure introduced to speed up the removal of popish 'images' and old service books. There was also a widespread movement (involving both clergy and laity) to extend the use of communion tables outside London. Before the next session was summoned in January 1552, those conservative bishops had been removed and Cranmer had revised his Prayer Book. In this way, the passage of reform bills was eased and, indeed, we see the beginnings of truly radical reform – a full-scale movement away from Catholic tradition.

The most important piece of legislation was the new enabling act – forcing the use of the second Book of Common Prayer (1552) – the rather more harshly penal second Act of Uniformity – supplemented by a new formulary of faith, the *Forty-Two Articles* (not strictly a parliamentary measure and never implemented). The new Uniformity Act and new Prayer Book condemned most of the traditional Catholic ceremonies, in line with continental Protestantism, and:

▶ rewrote the burial service

▶ altered the communion service (the old structure of the mass was abandoned along with many old prayers)

- ▶ dropped the word 'mass' in favour of 'Lord's Supper' or 'Holy Eucharist'
- ▶ abandoned old vestments in favour of a plain white surplices
- ▶ placed restrictions on singing
- ▶ used ordinary bread (now given into the communicant's hands)
- ▶ made attendance compulsory.

These were supplemented by a 'reformed' liturgy that featured a Calvinist Eucharistic doctrine ('spiritual' rather than 'physical' presence) and the infamous 'Black rubric' (which stated that kneeling at the communion table did not imply adoration of the host or real presence in any form). The second prayer book provided a system of worship based on scripture, with ceremonies suited to English tradition. To be sure that doctrinal reform succeeded, a new Treason Act outlawed questioning of either the royal supremacy or doctrinal innovations. On a somewhat less serious note, parliament also enacted legislation limiting the number of holy days to 25. Historians still debate one final reform proposal – a new initiative examining and restructuring church wealth.

This featured a new survey (in 1552) of episcopal temporal wealth, as well as all other clerical benefices with an income greater than fifty pounds, some of which would be transferred to the crown. It was suggested, for instance, that the bishopric of Durham be divided into two new sees – Durham and Newcastle – each with specific income allocations. The remaining £2,000 (from the original income) would then be available for crown purposes. With Bishop Tunstal in the Tower and too old to quarrel, it seemed there was little to halt the programme, except Edward's death. Whether this was a genuine reform effort (that is, a streamlining of church assets and division into more representative sees), a convenient financial initiative or mere aristocratic greed is something you will have to decide for yourself (although the second seems most reasonable).

What happened?

Dudley used the wealth reallocation scheme to solve some of those economic and social problems alluded to earlier, under Seymour. He knew that a rising gentry class would not forgo further opportunities to expand their own holdings at the expense of the church (making them dependent on continued reformation, like the married priests). Thus, after another episcopal re-evaluation:

- ▶ church properties were transferred into crown hands (and sold on)
- ▶ lead was confiscated (and put to other uses)
- ▶ bullion was coined from gold and silver plate.

The further secularisation of church property was, of course, little more than the continuation of an almost 20-year-old policy, like the selling of crown lands to ease debts. The end result was that the régime was able to make repayments on foreign loans on time and regularly and strengthen the domestic economy (indeed, benefiting both Mary and Elizabeth greatly). The problem, as should be obvious, is that much of this depends upon the continuation of Protestant reform. Edward's declining health and the fear of renewed Catholic power forced Dudley into more radical measures.

The importance of Lady Jane Grey

You are probably familiar with Jane, if only with the Hollywood version. She is sometimes known as the 'queen of nine days'. Unfortunately, she is more important for what she symbolises than for anything she actually did.

What did she symbolise?
Simply put, the continuation of the Reformation.

Most historians agree that, while Edward might not have been as sickly a youth as he is often portrayed, the undeniable fact is that, by early 1553, he was dying from pulmonary tuberculosis, an incurable disease. Clearly, while he liked the direction reform had been taking, no one doubted Mary would reverse it. Thus, although she was the rightful claimant (according to Henry VIII's will and the 1543 Act of Succession), it was thought necessary to bar her by whatever means possible. Dudley, with Edward's acquiescence, removed Mary (and Elizabeth and the Stuart succession) with letters patent on 21 June 1553. His daughters having been declared bastards, succession was passed to Henry VIII's great niece. When, on 6 July, Edward died, Jane was declared queen.

Why did this fail?
Three solid reasons explain Jane's (and Dudley's) failure:

▶ law
▶ loyalty
▶ bad public relations.

Briefly, Mary had been named heir by Henry VIII should Edward die without issue so few could accept that the succession could be altered as Dudley envisioned (despite Jane's religious beliefs). Moreover, though related to the Tudors, Jane was not a Tudor. On top of this, Dudley could not make the change look anything other than a grab for power (having married Jane off to his own son Guildford). Most telling, perhaps, was the fact that while Mary's religious leanings were well known, there was no real evidence that she was a 'papist', or that she had any intention of confiscating former church lands, or that she would not practice some form of religious toleration. In other words, when Edward died there were no reasons for Protestants to be afraid and, in short order, London proclaimed for Mary (19 July) and Dudley was arrested for treason (24 July).

Assessing the reign

This is difficult. While almost everything Seymour and Dudley tried came to naught, with regard to religion at least, something was achieved. Change took hold in many parts of the country, if only to the extent that most people were no longer, strictly speaking, dogmatic Catholics (but nor were they fanatical Protestants). At best, we can say that the English had become theologically ambivalent.

TUTORIAL

Summary of key ideas
▶ **Iconoclastic vandalism** – acts of wanton destruction against statues, images, paintings and other decorations.

▶ **Chantry(-ies)** – any endowment (in money or land) to a priest for the purpose of saying prayers for the soul of the founder.

▶ **Homilies** – sets of pre-prepared sermons on major issues or for specific occasions.

▶ **Enclosure(s)** – the practice of hedging off (fencing off) former open farmlands for the purpose of pasture.

Progress questions
1.   Why did the Seymour régime produce such limited reform?

2.   How was Dudley able to focus on further, more radical, reform?

Discussion points
1.   In what ways was reform more radical under Dudley than under Seymour?

2.   Did England emerge from the reign of Edward VI as a Protestant nation?

Practical assignment
You will probably encounter 'why-how type' questions (for example, 'Why were the regents not able to achieve more lasting reforms'?). There are two questions here – do you agree with the basic premise (e.g., can reform be described as radical?) and, consequently, what is your evidence? To prepare for such questions, decide now what keywords like 'radical', 'moderate' and 'lasting' actually mean, and make a chart listing various reform issues under these headings.

Study and revision tips
You might well be asked to write about Edwardian reform in an essay or in an exam. With this in mind, you should:

1. Create a chronological outline of the main events (c.1547–1553) with some commentary on the motivations of the main figures (Edward, Seymour, Dudley, Cranmer, etc.).

2. Create a thematic outline of the reign, divided under Seymour and Dudley, with a commentary on continuity, problems, and solutions (Protestant reform, revolts, the succession, etc.).

4

Mary I and Catholic Retrenchment

One-minute summary – Mary's reign was short and filled with incongruities. What began in glory ended ignominiously; she achieved most of her aims (religious or otherwise) although most were unpopular; she strove for internal stability but caused hardship and revolt. Traditional Catholic dogmas, doctrines and ceremonies were reinstated but, ultimately, they were made to look tyrannical and foreign. In the end, Mary's impact was small. This chapter will help you to understand:

▶ Mary's religious views
▶ the key issues and how these were resolved
▶ the role of parliament
▶ the influence of Gardiner and Pole
▶ the impact of the reign.

Assessing Mary's religious views

The problem is not her religious views which were clearly Catholic – it is rather in assessing her attitude. In various accounts she seems arrogant and greatly bigoted against Protestants or, conversely, as rather sympathetic, religiously tolerant, and easily led by her husband and ministers in dangerous directions. Indeed, she has been described, somewhere, by any adjective you could imagine. You will have to decide for yourself what truth, if any, these opinions may hold. Beyond contradiction, however, is the fact that almost all of her objectives had social and political ramifications of which she seemed unaware. Of course, she had been in near perpetual isolation since the early 1530s and, as a woman, had never been trained for leadership. Indeed, the reign was dogged by a question of legitimacy – the legal system was founded on the assumption of a ruling king.

What were her stated aims?
Mary took the overwhelming support shown for her after the death of her brother as an indication that the country wanted Roman Catholicism reinstated rather than the, perhaps, more obvious indication of loyalty to the legitimacy which she represented as a true Tudor. We cannot, with certainty, dismiss her interpretation, however. What we can say is that she set out to fulfil her aims (and what she took to be the country's desires) as quickly as possible, thinking that this would ensure stability. Clearly, most of her other aims (and the resulting problems) were connected to her original belief. In brief, these aims were:

▶ The restoration of papal obedience (including previous tax and tithe relations).
▶ The Spanish marriage.
▶ The resettlement of former church lands and properties.
▶ The abolition of Protestantism.

As you will see, other influences forced Mary into actions not initially contemplated – like harsh heresy laws and censorship.

How were these aims implemented?

As in previous reigns, Mary made sure that the message was entrusted into the hands of sympathetic authority figures (that is, bishops who could be trusted). One of the first things she did was to restore conservatives to their former positions. Thus, almost immediately, Gardiner was restored to Winchester and Bonner to London. In quick succession, other restorations followed:

▶ Nicholas Heath to Worcester.
▶ John Veysey (now 91) to Exeter (to be replaced the next year by James Turberville).

while, in other cases, radicals were deprived their sees and replaced with conservatives throughout 1554. For example:

▶ Maurice Griffen was appointed to Rochester.
▶ John Hopkin (Mary's confessor) was appointed to Norwich.

But, as in previous reigns, the majority of bishops simply remained in place – suggesting pliable religious opinions. John Scory, for instance, had married under Edward. Having renounced it and having repented, he remained at Chichester (only to flee England in 1556). The see of Worcester, left vacant by Heath's translation to York in 1555, saw the 'official' appointment of Richard Pates.

Now, interestingly, Pates had been bishop since 1541 (when he had been 'papally provided' with the see on the death of Jerome de'Ghinucci); as such, in 1547 he had attended the Council of Trent in that capacity. Along with Cardinal Reginald Pole, Mary's cousin and a religious exile since the late 1520s, Pates gave the régime a real connection to the international church and continental Catholic reformation. The deprived Protestant bishops were arrested and imprisoned or burnt as heretics (including, famously, Cranmer, Hooper and Ridley). With safe hands on the helm, Mary felt confident enough to proceed to parliament, initiate reform, and dream of her marriage.

What was the role of parliament?

As previous reigns had used parliament to both implement religious change and to lend them the appearance of widespread support, now only parliament could reverse or repeal the process. So, if Mary wanted Catholicism restored quickly and efficiently she had no choice but to summon parliament. The reign saw five parliaments:

5 October to 6 December 1553
2 April to 5 May 1554
12 November 1554 to 16 January 1555
21 October to 9 December 1555
20 January to 7 March 1558 (first session) and 5–17 November 1558 (second session dissolved by the death of Mary)

which is not to say they all dealt with religion, but most of them did touch upon the subject somehow. Nor should you read into this any kind of determined plan of action on Mary's part (besides restoration). Like previous Tudors, her aims were modified and remodelled by both internal and external influences, such as:

▶ Wyatt's rebellion
▶ Philip of Spain
▶ diplomatic negotiations
▶ factionalism
▶ Protestant resolve.

So that, in many ways, her régime was equally proactive and reactive. However, between 1553 and 1555 (when most of the important religious work was done), in effect, Catholicism was restored.

How was Catholicism restored?
The sessions of 1553 saw the abolishment of the Edwardian Reformation statutes through the first Act of Repeal. In essence, what this achieved was the restoration of the church's doctrinal position *circa* 1547 (as determined by the Act of Six Articles). You might well ask why Mary did not have parliament simply repeal all of the Henrician legislation of the 1530s too (like the dissolution of the monasteries). The truth is that at this point she dare not.

You are there ...
Put yourself in the place of a loyal aristocrat whose fortune and position rests on lands and profits your family made in the aftermath of the dissolutions. Would you support Mary if you knew she was going to reverse those acts and demand the return of former monastic properties? Would you want a role in the resulting administrative nightmare?

You are there ...
Conversely, as queen, you depend on the nobles and gentry, most of whom
have exploited previous church properties for personal gains. Knowing this,
would you ask them to return it, try to find a compromise or leave it unsettled
until a later date?

Some legislation aimed at rebuilding lost clerical authority and prestige was
implemented, but parliament was not completely subservient, however. At this
point, for example, it was too much to ask that church attendance be made
compulsory. Nor would parliament consider the restoration of the see of Durham
(for now obvious reasons of property and administrative difficulty). Mary had,
nonetheless, achieved restoration in religious terms and, perhaps for now, that was
enough.

Shortly thereafter, she made it plain (overriding Gardiner's objections) that she
would marry Philip of Spain and, thus, tie England into the Habsburg's worldwide
empire. The resultant uprisings meant that parliament's programme was greatly
curtailed until peace was restored. When it was recalled in 1554, Gardiner set out to
establish Mary's authority more firmly by the tried and tested method of expanded
heresy legislation. Unfortunately, his over-extensive programme was opposed by
Sir William Paget (an experienced politician who had not been in prison for the last
six years). Here we begin to see the 'Bloody Mary' of historical fame emerging (see
below). The period between the May and November sessions of 1554 also saw the
long-awaited return of Reginald Pole (also dealt with below).

Mary's third parliament saw the passage of the second Act of Repeal which,
finally, abolished the Henrician acts of the 1530s (including royal supremacy).
England was, officially, now reunited with Rome. It did not, however, mean the
restoration of all monastic lands. Mary had had to trade off success on the one hand
with guarantees that the aristocracy could keep their gains without fear of financial
penalty. She did return those monastic properties still in crown hands (a relatively
small percentage). At the same time, parliament also restored the old heresy laws.
Although, henceforth Protestants were burnt as heretics, this might not have turned
into the pogrom it did had it not been for the death of Gardiner in 1555.

Mary had not only lost a skilled lawyer, diplomat and her senior bishop, she had
also lost the voice of reason and caution. Gardiner realised early on that extensive
burnings would only strengthen Protestant resolve and encourage opposition from
the exiled Protestant community. It would, worst of all, make Catholicism look like
the religion of fanatics. How many Catholics, for instance, had been burnt under
Edward? Protestantism looked positively enlightened by comparison. Another
problem was who better than Gardiner knew the vicissitudes of the English as well
as the ins and outs of religious legislation, doctrinal reform and the problems of
translating this to the diocesan and parish levels? Well, certainly not Reginald Pole,
who had been cloistered in Rome since 1530 agitating against Lutheranism. In any

case, the 1554 and 1555 sessions of parliament saw the enactment of new treason legislation, dealing with the spread of seditious rumours and treason by words. Most of this could have been avoided had Mary heeded Gardiner's advice over Pole's.

Assessing the 'Spanish marriage'

One popular image of the queen is that she was near-fanatically obsessed with the idea of marriage to Philip of Spain. While the 'fanatic' label makes for great drama in Hollywood history films, there were practical advantages to the match for England. These include:

▶ A connection to the most powerful European state.
▶ A useful connection to England's most vital commercial partner (in that the Low Countries were part of Philip's inheritance).
▶ A connection to the real 'defender of the faith' (Emperor Charles V – Philip's father).

There is also the less tangible but, perhaps, psychologically significant, connection between the queen and the homeland of her mother, who had suffered so much for it.

You are there ...
Imagine yourself in Mary's place. For years you have faced political, social and emotional isolation because of your mother's connection to Spain and the Empire. Now, suddenly, these things count in your favour. Could you handle the sudden change in emotional circumstances? Might you not be a little 'fanatical' about it all?

Of course it is evident that such a close connection would have drawbacks too:

▶ involvement in Habsburg disputes on the continent
▶ accommodation with foreign authority over English subjects
▶ immediate hostility from France.

Indeed, these concerns fuelled Wyatt's rebellion.

Understanding Wyatt's rebellion

On 16 November 1553, the Commons had petitioned Mary to marry an Englishman, suggesting Edward Courtenay, Edward IV's great-grandson, as an ideal match. When Mary rejected this option, wheels were set in motion to force her hand. In essence, Philip's landing was to be prevented by a coordinated effort between concerned southern nobles and the French. By late January, however, Gardiner had uncovered the details (from Courtenay himself) and, thereafter, conspiracy related matters were rushed in the territories of the conspirators, most finding little support beyond a few Protestant die-hards and personal servants and bondsmen. Wyatt's Kentish power base, however, proved more resolute.

From 19 January, at Allington Castle near Maidstone, Wyatt plotted with trusted friends and raised his standard on the 25th, dismissing offers of negotiation and issuing proclamations of war. He was able to gather considerable sympathy for the anti-Spanish cause through an effective propaganda programme appealing to patriotism and the need to save Mary from 'evil councillors'. Of course, when the real plot to put Courtenay and Elizabeth on the throne was discovered, Wyatt's officers defected. Some Londoners still supported Wyatt, so he had an opportunity to win the day, provided the rest of London could be convinced. Mary stalled for time by offering a pardon and grievance discussions, which forced Wyatt to wait at Blackheath. Mary manoeuvred for the support and loyalty of London by painting her opponents as 'heretics', and successfully flattered her way into the affections of parliament. Most importantly, she kept her nerve.

Ultimately, with London's backing, she won the day. Perhaps because there had been such sympathies towards Wyatt's concerns, leniency was shown to the rebel leaders. As only 40 soldiers had died in the fighting and as little damage had been done otherwise, only a small number of rebels were executed. The one tangible result was that Gardiner's political rival, Paget, gained ground on him in Mary's eyes as a supporter of the Spanish match. Clearly, the political causes stand out, but there were religious elements to the rebellion, including:

▶ the sacking of the bishop of Winchester's palace and library (Gardiner represented all things Catholic and traditional)
▶ enthusiastic evangelicals making up the rebel leadership
▶ hints and rumours that former monastic lands would be forcibly returned.

Moreover, there was very real concern over Philip's intentions. What would he do if he and Mary produced an heir? Heaven forbid Mary should die in childbirth, but what if she did? What would be his real power?

Assessing the marriage
In the end, the rebels' concerns were addressed. The marriage treaty of 12 January 1554 featured the following points:

▶ only Englishmen would fill offices of church and state
▶ if Mary died without issue, Philip would have no claims on England at all.

Even the question of a title was never resolved and, in any case, it seems clear that Philip had little or no intention of remaining in England any longer than he had to. He probably saw the marriage anyway as little more than a dynastic measure to ensure continued pressure on Valois France. By July 1555 it was clear that no heir was forthcoming and, by October, Charles V had abdicated in favour of his brother (the Holy Roman Emperor, Ferdinand) and his son Philip who returned to take up his new responsibilities as King of Spain. He returned to England only once thereafter, in March 1556, to try to secure aid against the French, involving England once again in European conflicts (resulting in the loss of Calais on 13 January 1558). To his credit, while Mary lived, Philip tried to negotiate the return of Calais through the peace of Cateau-Cambresis (1559). When she died in November 1558, the condition was withdrawn. For all concerned, therefore, the marriage failed.

Bloody Mary

This is, without doubt, the most enduring image of any of the Tudors, superseded perhaps only by Elizabeth's 'virgin queen'. It is a negative image and, ultimately, the fault of Cardinal Pole.

The influence of Reginald Pole

The cardinal-legate arrived back in England in November 1554. He would have arrived sooner, had it not been for the aims and desires of Charles V, Philip of Spain and, to a certain extent, Mary herself.

From Mary's point of view, Pole could not be invited back into the country until she was sure that a diplomat of the Pope would be welcomed. She also knew that part of his demands for welcoming England back into the Roman fold was the return of monastic lands and properties (which would almost certainly cause another uprising). Some compromise had to be worked out before any official invitation was sent. That is not to say she and Pole did not regularly correspond over the many issues of Catholic reform and, Pole having been long in exile, English politics. In any case, Philip did not want him in the country until Catholicism was firmly back in place – he wanted to take credit for the achievement. Charles V supported his son and kept Pole awaiting permission to travel. Once Pole landed, he worked fast to further re-establish the church. He became Archbishop of Canterbury in December 1555, which aided his efforts considerably.

What were his aims?

His aims were largely identical to Mary's, including:

▶ the eradication of Protestantism in any form
▶ the re-establishment of the church's financial situation, c.1530
▶ better clerical education and discipline.

And, without the cautious influence of Gardiner, he made ground quickly, pursuing them with almost fanatical passion.

For example, it has been estimated that some 274 heretics were burnt after 1555 – making Mary's the harshest Catholic régime in Europe. As a consequence, the exiled community (largely in Geneva) increased dramatically, with the knock-on effect of many more anti-Catholic anti-Marian pamphlets flooding into England from abroad. Moreover, and more significant, is the fact that most of the burnt heretics had been very popular local preachers. Thus, in the minds of the people, Catholicism became inextricably linked with near tyrannical harassment (which itself became indelibly linked with Spain and Rome). Also, Pole was minded, despite the property compromise of 1555, to stabilise the church's finances and he ordered the founding of seminaries throughout the dioceses. The London Synod passed the Twelve Decrees (1555), which recognised the need for educated preachers and required bishops to regularly visit the parishes. So Pole had some limited success (if only he had had more time). Unfortunately, he was neither as sharp nor as charismatic as Gardiner and made significant errors:

▶ While opponents were censored, Pole never mounted or inspired a propaganda campaign in reply.

▶ He ordered the bishops and clergy into desired directions, but failed to inspire them to greater efforts.

▶ While he may have understood the spiritual ennui on the part of the laity (after so many acts and proclamations), he entirely ignored them in his pursuit of administrative efficiency.

▶ Most importantly, he rejected an offer for aid from the Jesuits (1555).

To paraphrase Robert Tittler; Pole knew that the English reformation had been a top-down process from the start, so he intended a rebuilding of the Catholic faith to be a similar top [the clergy] down [the laity] process. Having badly misread the current situation, however, for the first time a Tudor reign witnessed demonstrations against the burning of heretics.

Other social concerns

The ill will generated by the heresy issue was exacerbated by the severe lack of charitable institutions. Clearly, when the reforming statutes of previous régimes had dismantled this traditional staple of Catholic doctrine (the importance of charity and good works), they forgot to replace it with some other device. Had the Marian régime lasted longer, the problem might have solved itself through the re-establishment of monastic and secular charitable institutions. What the régime did accomplish was not unimpressive but the measures taken were simply not meant to be long-term. These include:

▶ The granting of more charters of incorporation (giving local authorities the power to deal with local concerns as they saw fit).

► The re-distribution of grain from areas of surplus to areas of scarcity.
► The appointment of justices of the peace as poor-law overseers.
► Re-examination of the tillage-enclosure question weighted in favour of farmers.

And, while these measures did not completely solve the problem, they gave Elizabeth a firm basis upon which to build in the next reign.

TUTORIAL

Summary of key ideas
► **The Spanish marriage** – the marriage of Mary and Philip of Spain which re-established past connections and commitments.

► **The restoration of papal obedience** – this was Mary's aim of re-establishing Roman Catholic hegemony in England and, consequently, abolishing royal supremacy.

► **The Council of Trent** – an ecumenical church council which met at times between 1545 and 1563 to refine Catholic doctrine, discipline and papal authority.

► **Bloody Mary** – an epithet that conveys the enduring image of Mary as a Catholic fanatic in pursuit of Protestant heretics.

Progress questions
1.   How was Mary able to achieve her stated aims so quickly and efficiently?

2.   Why was the Spanish marriage such a difficult issue?

Discussion points
1.   At the end of Mary's reign, was England Catholic once again?

2.   Was Gardiner or Pole Mary's more influential advisor?

3.   Why could Mary not pursue a full restoration of monastic lands?

Practical assignment
You will probably encounter 'comparison type' questions (for example, 'Was the Spanish Marriage good or bad for England?') where you will be asked to weigh options and justify your opinions; there are no correct answers! To prepare, make a chart of three columns, labelled 'issues' (marriage, papal obedience, new heresy laws, etc.), 'positive results' and 'negative results'.

Study and revision tips
You might well be asked to write about Marian reforms in an essay or in an exam.

With this in mind, you should:

1.   Create a chronological outline of the main events (c.1553–1558) with some commentary on the motivations of the main figures (Mary, Gardiner, Pole, etc.)

2.   Create a thematic outline of the reign, with commentary on both the problems encountered (like declining charity) and solutions tried (like grain redistribution).

Elizabeth I – The Settlement

One-minute summary – Elizabeth wanted domestic stability. One way to ensure this was through a broad-based national church that would have widespread appeal and occasion no religious controversy. It would be truly unique in that a Calvinist theology would paper over a Catholic hierarchy and ceremonial structure. To achieve her aims, Elizabeth had to perform a remarkable balancing act between competing, and often compelling, spiritual pressures. This chapter will help you to understand:

▶ Elizabeth's own religious views
▶ the Religious Settlement of 1559
▶ the roles of parliament and of leading church figures
▶ the views and influence of the Puritan and Catholic sects.

The influence of Elizabeth

Elizabeth had moderate Protestant views and strove to avoid serious spiritual conflicts. The circumstances surrounding her birth, upbringing – in the household of Catherine Parr (a devout Protestant) – and education at the hands of Matthew Parker, perhaps made this attitude inevitable.

Why was she not more fanatical about religion?
A good question, and historians offer up three useful explanations:

▶ history
▶ political necessity
▶ domestic tranquillity.

Keep in mind that she had witnessed fanaticism in the previous two reigns and knew first hand the potential dangers. Moreover, England was at war with France and could not afford to alienate Philip II and the Pope by ditching Mary's Catholicism too hastily. Nor did she wish to alienate many of her own subjects who were committed Catholics. Finally, she strongly believed that doctrine was a matter for herself and her clerical advisors alone (although, initially, parliament had to be consulted too).

What did she want?
In essence:

- ▶ a Protestant church
- ▶ with as widespread an appeal as possible
- ▶ as inoffensive to Catholics as possible.

The religious settlement was meant to provide all of these things. Elizabeth had one advantage in that, since the 1530s, people had lost interest in theological and doctrinal niceties. For most people, religion had become mere ritual. Thus, the Catholicism facing Elizabeth was local in nature and reinforced by regional customs. The settlement was not, therefore, attacking religion *per se*, but disunity.

The religious settlement, 1559

To understand fully the settlement and its ramifications for the entire country, we must pause to consider its constituent parts. Four statutes were introduced into Elizabeth's first parliament. They dealt with:

- ▶ supremacy
- ▶ uniformity
- ▶ religious taxation
- ▶ use of church property.

Supremacy
The new bill rejected papal authority in whatever form, transferring these powers to Elizabeth. Oddly, this, and the title of Supreme Head were both fiercely resisted by the parliamentarians. She had to settle for the title 'Supreme Governor'. Why?

- ▶ To devout Protestants, only Christ could be 'Head' of the church in any real and meaningful way.

- ▶ The Bible severely restricted female religious authority.

- ▶ Catholics could not accept the monarch as 'Head' of the Church.

- ▶ It implied that she was exercising authority over the church in the name of Christ – not under her own authority.

Did a slightly altered title make any real practical difference? Probably not; Elizabeth was fully determined that the final authority in any matter would be hers and hers alone, but:

- ▶ Protestants would be more than happy to leave the spectre of papal supremacy behind, and

▶ Catholics would be able to accept this less radical option, as their loyalties to Elizabeth would not be too seriously compromised thereby.

In addition, the new bill repealed the Marian heresy laws, which beyond doubt had created more problems than solutions, and it reinforced many traditional Catholic practices. It also included a loyalty oath, established a High Commission to enforce it, and ordered all roods be replaced with the royal arms.

Uniformity
By now uniformity was a familiar issue. Elizabeth's church would be Protestant, but which option would be pursued?

1. Lutheranism would give Elizabeth allies among the German princes – similar to the 1549 settlement.

2. Calvinism would please returning Marian exiles and provide a strong and increasingly popular doctrinal underpinning – similar to the 1552 settlement.

3. The Henrician situation, c.1547, would allow a balanced view between these extremes and Rome.

For maximum effect, Elizabeth opted for a blending of all three. Services would be conducted according to the 1552 book (with some alterations, c.1549) while certain 'Catholic' traditions and ceremonies would be retained and enforced.

What were these alterations?
In brief:

▶ any statements (c.1552) critical of, or insulting to, the Pope were removed (to avoid unnecessary political tension and aggravation);

▶ the 'black rubric' was omitted (review Chapter 3);

▶ it reinforced the 1549 recommended usages of ornaments and vestments (to re-enforce traditional practices);

▶ it featured a combined statement on the spiritual value of the Mass.

The last point bears closer inspection.
Recall that Catholics and Lutherans accepted a 'real' presence, whereas Calvinists accepted only a 'spiritual' or 'commemorative' presence. By combining statements from the 1549 and 1552 prayer books, albeit imprecisely, either belief could read into the new wording. Moreover, non-attendance on Sundays and holy days was made subject to a twelve pence fine. The most controversial aspect of this part of the settlement, however, was the so-called Ornaments Rubric, which:

▶ enforced the use of crosses, candlesticks and other traditional furnishings
▶ enforced the use of the alb, cope and a surplice.

We shall examine why this was so controversial in due course.

Religious taxation and church property

For reasons more practical than spiritual, the revenues derived from First Fruits and Tenths (see Chapter 1) were restored to the crown. This was followed up by the dissolution of those monasteries and chantries founded by Mary. As earlier, the gentry would be happy to see more church property become available (as well as having previous gains safeguarded). But the question of usage was wider than this, of course. The Act of Exchange allowed the crown (during times of episcopal vacancy) to award to the sees any recently acquired spiritual revenues (like tenths or tithes) in exchange for its temporal assets (manors, parks, forests, etc.). Moreover, the bishops could no longer lease out properties for periods of more than 21 years (accept to the crown). In theory, this assured that the value of church property would keep pace with inflation. In other words, when the crown finally acquired them, the lands would not be undervalued.

How could the Marian bishops accept all this?

Simply put, they could not, nor were they alone in opposition. Besides the Marian bishops and some other Catholic campaigners, some historians point to a radical Protestant tendency among certain parliamentarians (although recently, this claim has lost many adherents). There were probably some radicals (there always are), but most members would probably support whatever government legislation was introduced (concerned, as they were, mainly with recent property gains). As a result, the first session of parliament achieved little and the government bills (far harsher than those ultimately passed) became so truncated that only the new title was approved. Even so, the Lords refused to make the title official, leaving Elizabeth's authority open to question. And, without clear and legal powers, her settlement would be merely tenuous, resulting in instability and, potentially, violence. To get around the bishops' opposition, it was necessary to intimidate them into acceptance or, at least, humiliate them into standing down.

How was this achieved?

Elizabeth staged a public disputation between the Protestant and Catholic divines at Westminster Abbey shortly before parliament's second session (recalled in April). Rigged as it was against the Catholic divines, they withdrew, giving Elizabeth an excuse for arresting bishops Watson (Lincoln) and White (Winchester) for disobedience. Thereby, the second session saw a subdued Catholic leadership, now a numerical minority in the Lords. What opposition remained was appeased by the queen's acceptance of certain compromises (those rites and ceremonies mentioned above).

Were there any other problems?

Yes. The Marian bishops did not simply capitulate. They all, save Anthony Kitchen of Llandaff (now in his 80s), refused the new supremacy oath. Of course, this gave Elizabeth the opportunity to deprive them of their sees and fill the vacancies with Protestants. Sadly, the necessity of filling vacancies with divines from the exile community led to two additional problems.

First, while Elizabeth might be satisfied that the religious question had been solved – she had achieved her goals – the new bishops and other Protestant divines were not satisfied, seeing the settlement as only a necessary, and severely flawed, first step down the long road toward Geneva. They were anxious to remove every trace of 'papal' influence and wanted revenge for their treatment under Mary. Second, some of the best theologians refused to accept bishoprics, and had to be coerced. Clearly, by appointing men to positions of authority who were much more committed to radical reform than she was, Elizabeth faced potential schism at every turn.

You are there ...

Imagine yourself a returning exile. In Geneva, you witnessed first hand a successful, interwoven Protestant society. There were no bishops and no papal rites and ceremonies. There was a firm biblical foundation for every element. The salvation of the soul was assured to the worthy – the elect. In England, this was not the case and Elizabeth was satisfied. Would you accept this or do everything you could to assure the salvation of your family and countrymen, even if it meant opposing Elizabeth?

How were these changes enforced?

As before, a new Act of Uniformity was followed up by royal injunctions and a royal visitation. You should be familiar with the concept of injunctions by now and the 1559 was very similar to the 1547 set, including:

▶ orders that the clergy perform their duties as laid out in the settlement;
▶ recommendations for the elimination of idolatry (without wanton destruction!);
▶ the prohibiting of pilgrimages;
▶ the maintaining of clerical marriages (with a few additional regulations).

What was unexpected was that this set also enforced many traditional practices and reinforced the conservative modifications lately made to the Prayer Book. They included such things as:

▶ a clerical dress code
▶ traditional forms of music
▶ the use of unleavened bread
▶ the retaining of certain traditional images.

It was also Elizabeth's intention that the injunctions be used to improve educational standards across the board and, with this in mind, pushed for 'monthly' sermons. Of course, in many ways radical Protestant bishops, those responsible for the visitations that followed on 19 July, were not happy with many of these provisions and simply ignored what they did not like, or enforced more vigorously those they did. The result was that:

▶ Some 400 clergymen either resigned or were deprived their livings over the next five years.
▶ There was greater destruction of material objects than Elizabeth envisioned.
▶ There was greater local variation in practice.
▶ The sermon, rather than the Mass, became the central element in many locations.

Elizabeth decided that some of the visitors had gone too far and demanded, at least, that a crucifix be retained in every church. The bishops saw even this as reminiscent of papal error and some prepared to resign over the issue. Elizabeth capitulated, but kept the crucifix in the Chapel Royal (where it would be seen by foreign dignitaries who might have questioned her faith). By 1560, having largely got her way, Elizabeth left the bishops to get on with the task of administration.

Assessing the influence of leading churchmen

Elizabeth had her settlement. Did demands for further reform disappear? Did all discussion of religious issues fade into insignificance? Obviously not, but Elizabeth assumed that difficulties would be handled by the bishops according to the settlement statutes. However, in the early 1560s negotiations ended the war with France. Once again, therefore, the Catholic powers were free to focus on England. Elizabeth needed the bishops to stand firm.

Assessing Parker and his *Thirty-nine Articles*
Her first Archbishop of Canterbury was her former tutor Matthew Parker. He was familiar, a former Catholic and considered a 'safe pair of hands'. He was vigorously committed to moderate reform, and earned the epithet 'nosy Parker' for his in-depth investigations. Although he might have wished to go further, Parker implemented the settlement as it was, monitored abuses, and acted against non-settlement-based practices. In 1563, the *Thirty-Nine Articles* – a definitive statement of church doctrine – was developed in convocation as a guide. It heavily favoured

Calvinism, including such statements as:

- '...Holy Scripture containeth all things necessary to salvation' (art.vi)
- '...no power to do good works pleasant and acceptable to God' (art.x)
- '...we are justified by faith alone' (art.xi)
- '...two sacraments Baptism, and the Supper of the Lord' (art.xxv)
- '...Transubstantiation cannot be proved by Holy Writ' (art.xxviii).

At a stroke, every 'popish' rite, ceremony or tenet of faith was eliminated. It would unsettle every Catholic in the country and powerful Catholics abroad. Elizabeth withheld official sanction and refused to allow parliament to confirm them. She did not disapprove of the 'theology' *per se* – clearly the church was 'unofficially' Calvinist in many ways already. It had to appear to welcome Catholics too, which was why the settlement insisted on 'traditional' rites, ceremonials and furnishings. Therein lay another problem.

The Vestiarian Controversy (January 1565)
By 1563, two Oxford dons – Laurence Humphrey and Thomas Sampson – had made their protests too public. They refused to wear the surplice and cope, and they protested over the injunctions' prescription of distinctive outdoor clerical dress. In response, Parker issued the *Advertisements* (in 1566), a statement of doctrines, prayers and sacraments, ordering traditional clerical costume. This ignited a wider protest and sackings followed. It also brought official attention to the existence of a more radical Protestant group in the capital. While Parker may have considered dress codes merely adiaphora (i.e., 'things indifferent'), Puritans considered untenable anything not based in scripture. All told, Parker was effective and eased the settlement into hearts and minds. Sadly, Edmund Grindal did not follow suit.

Assessing the work of Archbishop Grindal (1575-83)
Grindal had been Bishop of London (later Archbishop of York) during the recent dress controversy and had tried to take a sympathetic approach. He had also taken a gentle approach to the enforcement of the last injunctions. Much admired as a churchman, he was politically naive. As archbishop, he made two serious errors in judgement.

- He allowed the publication of the Geneva Bible.
- He supported prophesying.

The Geneva Bible
Parker had either deliberately suppressed this version or had at least blocked its importation. Grindal, however, with the support of leading noblemen, approved its publication for personal and domestic use by the laity, and approved special editions for the lectern in parish churches. This irritated Elizabeth as she had supported the *Bishops Bible*, the approved text, with which the Geneva version now

competed and, in many cases, supplanted (upsetting the settlement and uniformity statutes). Some later editions even contained a revised Prayer Book, eliminating all those remaining 'popish' elements. This was a minor irritant for Elizabeth, however, when compared to Grindal's other misjudgement.

What are prophesyings?

In brief, these are unauthorised meetings for prayers, discussions and preaching practice, where would-be preachers learned the profession – reading biblical passages, debating interpretations and judging lay responses to their techniques. Now, this may seem innocent enough, but Elizabeth thought differently.

Picturing the scene ...

Elizabeth considered the religion question settled. Priests learn their trade in the universities. The Bible and theology is interpreted only by bishops and divines in convocation and according to the settlement. Priests should preach the same message and read from the same approved books of homilies and prayers throughout the realm. As queen, would you not be concerned to learn that there were men preaching unscripted sermons in an impromptu fashion? Would you think such gatherings dangerous to the health of the church and, potentially, of the nation? What would you do about them?

Elizabeth demanded these meetings be squashed, and she expected Grindal to handle it immediately. She was concerned that Catholic activists would take the opportunity to stir up trouble (examined below). In 1576, Grindal was ordered to suppress them, but he saw them as useful educational tools and refused to do so. Prophesying helped the laity to understand the tenets of the faith, and helped ministers (not priests) to develop effective preaching styles. He argued that, in any case, the laity was not included in the subsequent analysis sessions, so what was the problem? He then, unwisely, took two additional steps. He canvassed episcopal opinion on the issue and found that at least ten of his colleagues agreed with him. He then followed up with a letter to Elizabeth, explaining that:

▶ prophesyings were good
▶ she was only the highest 'political' authority in the land and that she too had to defer to the will of God (which only divines could fully appreciate).

Try to imagine how angry Elizabeth must have been over Grindal's defiance. He was suspended from his office (he could not be legally deprived of it) and remained under house arrest from the summer of 1577 to his death in 1583. In essence, the church was without a primate for six years. He was finally replaced by John Whitgift (Bishop of Worcester since 1577).

Assessing the work of Archbishop Whitgift (1583–1604)

Whitgift was harsh and uncompromising but shared all the views and aspirations for the church of his sovereign. He distrusted Puritans and Catholics alike, and demanded obedience to the settlement as enacted. Elizabeth called him her 'little black husband'. Almost his first undertaking as archbishop was the promulgation of three acts for the clergy to subscribe.

▶ An acknowledgement of the royal supremacy.

▶ A pledge of support for the Prayer Book and Ordinal (as enacted).

▶ A pledge of support for the *Thirty-Nine Articles* (given official sanction in 1570).

As a result, some 400 ministers lost their preaching licences (although compromises were made, there being too few replacements) and the presses were effectively muzzled. Indeed, in 1585, Puritan and, in particular, Presbyterian complaints were effectively silenced by articles promulgated against them in convocation (examined below). If churchmen were giving Elizabeth grief, sadly, she got no relief from her parliaments.

Assessing the influence of parliament

In the first instance, as you are aware, Elizabeth had no choice but to approach religious reform through parliament. Religion (both in terms of supremacy and uniformity) was enshrined in statute, and only crown and parliament working together could amend or remove existing statutes. As you are also aware, once the settlement was so enshrined, Elizabeth considered the matter closed. Parliament, however, did not.

Why didn't Parliament accept the settlement?

This is a good question; one with several answers. In brief, the members could not understand why they were to be silent on this issue, because:

▶ they had been involved in the determination of spiritual matters since the 1530s;

▶ the issue of domestic tranquillity was equally important to them as concerned individuals;

▶ the aristocracy had made great material gains in recent years and were determined to protect them.

Moreover, we cannot simply ignore the possibility that some members were genuinely committed to further reform. And, by refusing to allow parliament to comment on anything but the most peripheral issues, political instability remained a potential threat. In any case, reform suggestions were made, but were limited to issues of abuses in the church.

What did parliament do?
In reality, little more than Elizabeth would allow. Three Acts go a long way toward illustrating this point. These were:

▶ The 1581 Act against reconciliation with Rome (in response to Catholic plots) which established a punitive fine for failing to attend services.

▶ The 1593 Act against popish Recusants (they were confined to specific geographical areas).

▶ The 1593 Act against Protestant sectarians (largely a repeat of the Recusant Act, except with the option of exile).

Besides these marginally necessary statutes, we have only some minor acts to consider otherwise.

The 1571 Treason Act modified the supremacy bill by making it treasonous to say that Elizabeth was a heretic or a schismatic, although it otherwise repeated earlier Acts. Added to this was the 1571 Act against Bulls from Rome, and the 1585 Act 'for the provision to be made for the surety of Elizabeth's most royal person' – a response to the activities of Jesuit and seminary priests (examined below). In essence, any man ordained under the authority of Rome after 1558 was adjudged a traitor. Of course, parliament discussed the major issues too, but it is testimony to Elizabeth's will that they successfully legislated on so few of them.

Assessing the influence of Protestant and Catholic malcontents

By now you should be comfortable with the meaning of such terms as 'Protestant' and 'Catholic'. Indeed, real interpretive problems only occur when we break them down into sub-categories and try to apply these as labels. For example, historians talk about Elizabeth's problems with 'Puritans' and 'Recusants'. These labels require some explanation.

Who were the Puritans?
We need only refer to three points. They were:

▶ committed Calvinists

▶ Geneva-centric on church/state and social control issues (i.e., they wanted to enforce an Old Testament mentality and morality)

▶ venomously anti-Catholic (i.e., they wanted to purge the church of all its 'papist' trappings).

But 'Puritan' was a term of abuse cast at those Protestants who could not, or would not, conform to the settlement. Historians have identified three types of Puritan, each of which deserves some examination:

▶ conformists
▶ Presbyterians
▶ separatists.

What does 'conformist' mean?

Recall that Parker and some Puritans disagreed over the significance of such things as clerical dress codes. Conformist Puritans agreed with Parker on such issues. Provided that those issues explicitly dealt with in scripture – like the Sacraments – were handled on a scriptural basis, they were content. Those things not mentioned – clerical dress and church government – they were content to let the authorities handle as they saw fit. The conformists probably realised that reform had gone as far as it was going to, and they made the best of it. And, provided they attended services and did not agitate for further reforms, Elizabeth let them be. Obviously, her letter to Parker of 1565, the Vestiarian Controversy and Advertisements of 1566 proved that there were plenty of non-conformists to worry about anyway. Those who gave far more serious opposition we know as 'Presbyterians'.

What does 'Presbyterian' mean?

The term stems from a belief system that holds that a church governed by bishops and priests is a papist error. Presbyterianism looks to Geneva, with its ministers and elders (or presbyters), as the true form. They agitated for Geneva-esque reform. Recall Grindal's support of prophesying; that would be an example of Presbyterian improvement.

An important Cambridge don – Thomas Cartwright – used his lectures on the New Testament to emphasise where the English church failed to meet biblical standards. He blamed the existing hierarchy and everything needed to support it. While this does not seem too radical, perhaps, his vice-chancellor – John Whitgift – queried Cartwright's opinions and finally got him sacked. Cartwright probably grew more radical as a result and, by June 1572, had influenced two others – John Field and Thomas Wilcox – to publish a pamphlet. The *Admonition* called for the immediate institution of Geneva-like pastors, deacons and elders in place of the bishops and priests (who they blamed for all non-scriptural church practices). This initiated a serious pamphlet debate, with men like Whitgift writing against them. Where conformists conformed, Presbyterians tended to agitate.

> **You are there ...**
> As queen, who would you see as the greater threat? Those who resented
> wearing the cope and surplice, who wanted to dress in a way which did not
> separate them from their congregations, or those who agitated for the
> complete removal of the episcopal system, the system upon which the royal
> supremacy was based?

Not only did the Presbyterians shock both queen and government, which reacted
by muzzling the printing presses and imprisoning the leaders (Field and Wilcox),
but they also shocked their fellow Puritans who were trying to achieve gradual
reform through proposed legislation. In men like Cartwright they saw only dire
consequences for their own minor reform proposals. You might wonder why more
was not done against them. There are a number of good explanations.

▶ Their movement was local, rather than national, in nature (and somewhat
   underground, like the prophesiers).

▶ They had powerful patrons at the highest levels of government.

▶ External matters, like the counter-Reformation, distracted officialdom from
   these relatively minor internal problems.

And, as we shall see, Catholicism was becoming a more serious threat to security in
the 1570s anyway. However, while the government might support a hands-off
attitude toward them, the bishops, for obvious reasons, did not. With the support of
Elizabeth and Parker, they closed down the presses, revoked preaching licences and
imprisoned Presbyterian leaders wherever they could be found. The death of Parker
and promotion of Grindal, however, saw a moratorium placed on Presbyterian
persecution.

With Grindal ineffective (post-1577), the bishops were free to continue their
offensive, precipitating the rather comical situation of Protestant bishops focusing
their energies on Protestant reformers while, at the same time, ignoring very real
and dangerous threats from radical Catholics. The government and other lay
authorities, however, saw the real threat and blocked the episcopal pogrom,
reasoning that all Protestant energy should be directed against Rome which, if little
else, guaranteed Presbyterian survival. Indeed, by the early 1580s we can see the
foundations of the so-called Classical Movement (Patrick Collinson, *The Elizabethan
Puritan Movement*, 1967), a more moderate alternative development.

What was the Classical Movement?
It was a local, grass-roots organisation of informal meetings and semi-formal
regional assemblies and synods. Like the prophesyings, like-minded individuals
gathered together to discuss issues of mutual importance. Sadly, a more radical sub-
sect took form.

Recall John Field. He saw in the movement an embryonic national system of synods that could by-pass episcopal authority, and he meant to use it. By 1584, he was confident enough to try to use the movement to influence parliamentary elections and, thereafter, get more radical reform statutes passed, eventually overturning the hated settlement. While petitions and surveys were carried out members of parliament were pressured to introduce a Geneva prayer book and church governmental system. Their ultimate influence was, however, minimal. The death of Grindal and the promotion of Whitgift were serious blows to Field's dreams. Through Whitgift's three articles (1583) and convocation's reform articles (1585), much Presbyterian thunder was stolen. While, as mentioned, some 400 preachers lost their licences, most others conformed to the settlement. Men like Field, however, do not give up easily.

A Presbyterian MP named Anthony Cope presented a bill in 1587 (possibly under Field's influence) calling for serious reform initiatives. Ultimately, it was far too radical for serious consideration, nor would Elizabeth budge from her belief that parliament had no voice in doctrinal issues, but for a time it was given serious consideration. Anti-Catholic feeling had been running high due to the discovery of the so-called Babington Plot (see below). But, with political support rapidly evaporating, men like Field and Cope focused their efforts instead on developing, what Doran called, a local 'shadow Church' instead. The Presbyterian movement, for all of its self-imposed localism, however, was effectively killed off by 1590. How?

▶ Most of its powerful patrons were dead.
▶ Divine right arguments for episcopal government were gaining credence.
▶ There were more successful episcopal efforts.
▶ Star Chamber trials (usually reserved for traitors) for the leadership.
▶ The Marprelate Tracts of 1588 and 1589.

What were the Marprelate Tracts?
These were a series of dialogues between two self-important, pompous and, ultimately, rather vulgar Presbyterian leaders criticising the bishops. The pamphlets made the Presbyterians look like fools, and scared away any further patronage. The bishops, the provisional targets of the tracts, seized the opportunity to portray the Presbyterians in the worst possible light, and with the leaders arrested and imprisoned, local classes dispersed. Did Martin Marprelate exist? No. Who wrote the tracts? Good question.

What does 'separatist' mean?
In light of the persecutions and Elizabeth's unwillingness to initiate further reform, many radicals simply gave up on the established church. To them, it would never be a 'godly' institution and, thus, they had best create their own. Recall that small, local and underground groups had been discovered recently in London. What remained of these now formed the nucleus of a new church. Like the other sects,

however, it did not last long. The bishops were easily able to uncover the members, and the leadership was eliminated in short order. Perhaps most damaging, however, was the attack on their position by Richard Hooker's *Of the Laws of Ecclesiastical Polity*.

In brief, Hooker's attack was effective because he emphasised many convincing points.

▶ He laid the emphasis on tradition and continuity.

▶ He de-emphasised preaching as the central feature in favour of the Eucharist.

▶ He advocated *via-media* between Rome and Geneva (much after the settlement).

▶ He rehearsed popular arguments about episcopal government and divine law.

However, that Puritanism managed to survive as well as it did into the seventeenth century is testament to the efforts and beliefs of the tiny groupings that remained in a kind of semi-autonomous conformity to the settlement.

What were Catholic Recusants?
Simply put, those Catholics who refused to attend established churches. But, all things considered, they were not really much of a problem.

Why weren't Recusants a problem?
Elizabeth had made it clear in 1559 that she was not interested in forcing dogma on to her Catholic subjects. What she wanted was to persuade them to conform either through a settlement which was not too radically different from existing Catholic beliefs or through mild financial penalties for not conforming. Measures included:

▶ a mild fine of twelve pence for non-attendance
▶ a fine of 100 marks (c.£33) for attending a Catholic Mass
▶ loss of office for Catholic clergy who refused to take the oath of supremacy
▶ the death penalty for saying or arranging a Mass.

Obviously, the fines were never enough to wipe a family out, but they were harsh enough to inspire serious considerations. If they wished to carry out their religion at home and in secret, provided they attended the established church too, Elizabeth was not particularly concerned. Moreover, the death penalty was not implemented until the late 1570s either. Like the Puritans, provided they were loyal, Catholics were free to believe what they wished. Some die-hards went to France in self-exile, but most remained.

Those who stayed were attended by non-permanently based priests in semi-formal gatherings (usually in noble houses) in the south, while some priests carried on much as they had done in the more remote northern and Welsh regions. It was believed, and rightly so, that most Catholics would slip into conformity over time. Few martyrs to the cause were created and, when arrests were made, it was only for high profile cases involving flagrant defiance of the settlement. Had it not been for serious and unforeseen disturbances to this peace, starting in the late 1560s, Catholicism might well have simply faded into the background. Problems were caused by:

▶ The conclusion of the Council of Trent and the implementation of its reforms (1563) on the continent.

▶ Mary Stuart's self-exile in England (1568) – as the obvious Catholic heir to the throne, this was viewed very seriously indeed.

▶ The revolt of the Northern Earls (1568).

▶ Pius V's excommunication of Elizabeth (1570).

▶ The Ridolfi (1571), Throckmorton (1583), and Babington (1586) plots to overthrow the settlement and reinstate Catholicism.

▶ The St Bartholemew's Day massacre (1572).

▶ The Douai priests (1573).

▶ The Jesuits (1580).

▶ The assassination of William of Orange (1584).

▶ The recurring question of the succession.

Now, we will not examine all these issues here, but you should familiarise yourself with them anyway. A brief word on a couple should suffice.

Who were the Northern Earls?

The Earls of Northumberland and Westmorland were dissatisfied with their lot in Elizabethan England (largely due to political enmity with the Cecils) and made contacts with Rome and Spain hoping to improve their fortunes. They pledged military support for a proposed marriage between Mary Stuart and the Duke of Norfolk (the most powerful Catholic noble) and hoped to reinstall Catholicism too. The plot was uncovered and Norfolk vehemently denied everything. The Earls had marched on Durham and forced a few changes in the Cathedral, but leading Catholic families failed to support them. The fact that English Catholics never joined or supported 'revolts' against Elizabeth says much for her original strategy of persuasion. Even the Pope's excommunication order was largely ignored.

What were the Ridolfi, Throckmorton and Babington Plots?

Generally, these were schemes aimed at promoting the interests of Mary Stuart and/or for the reinstallation of Catholicism. Norfolk, having avoided trouble, continued to pursue these aims through various means, while Mary wanted to return to Scotland at the, metaphorical, head of an army. Shortly after the excommunication, Norfolk's circle became involved with Roberto di Ridolfi, a London-based Florentine banker with connections to every major Catholic power. He promised them much (including the support of the Duke of Alva) if only Norfolk was prepared to make a request for assistance (i.e. commit treason) and raise his own troops in support when Alva landed. This plot was also uncovered and Norfolk executed.

Obviously, Mary Stuart was a focus for Catholic resentment in England, and an inspiration for Catholics abroad. The idea of Mary on the English throne, however, was the last thing Philip of Spain wanted (her connections to France were too strong), but political reality never seemed to occur to any of the English conspirators. The problem was clear to certain royal councillors, however, and they wanted Mary executed or, at least attainted (charged with treason) and excluded from the English succession. Elizabeth refused to do anything, except keep Mary sequestered. Again, she most likely feared the reaction of James VI of Scotland and the continental Catholic powers. Even the massacre of the Huguenots on St Bartholomew's Day failed to move Elizabeth to accept the idea of an international Catholic plot. But there were real threats.

In 1580, the Pope put out what can only be called 'a contract' on Elizabeth's head, assuring any potential assassins that the deed would be considered a 'good work'. Elizabeth dismissed this as utter nonsense until the assassination of William of Orange in 1584. Added to this was the discovery of the Throckmorton Plot, which involved Mary Stuart, the Duke of Guise and various English and Scottish Catholic malcontents. The final straw for Elizabeth, however, occurred in 1586 when Mary disinherited her son in favour of Philip of Spain (potentially securing his support). Mary had also been in correspondence with Anthony Babington, and endorsed his plan to help her escape prison and murder Elizabeth. Fortunately, the entire correspondence was filtered through Elizabeth's loyal advisors, and the plot was foiled. It appears that Elizabeth was then tricked into signing Mary's death warrant. You will have to decide the truth of this claim yourself. While one source of instability was thereby removed, others filled the vacuum.

The influence of the Douai priests and the Jesuits

Despite growing evidence that English Catholics would not support plots and schemes against their queen, Elizabeth could really have had little foundation left for maintaining that Catholicism would slowly dwindle away. Such an opinion could only have been confirmed by reports of priests and Jesuits being shipped into England in the 1580s.

Who were the Douai priests?

The lesser threat came from these missionaries. An English Catholic exile, William Allen, had established a seminary at Douai, in the Netherlands, in 1568 to provide a solid Catholic education for other exiles. The college became especially devoted to training priests to send back to England to rekindle the faith and convert the heretics. Allen, much after the Tridentine canons, emphasised bible study and preaching techniques so that the priests could meet their Protestant opponents on an equal footing. No doubt, the missionaries would have been more successful had it not been for the fact that they were ordered to steer clear of politics (when, clearly, the two went hand in hand). Of course, continuous papal efforts to mount a crusade against Elizabeth from either Spain, the Netherlands or from Ireland made their claims of political non-involvement seem utterly fantastic. This, and the fact that time and numbers counted against them (as did some 63 arrests and executions of their leaders). The introduction of Jesuits made matters worse.

Why did the Jesuits make the situation worse?

Elizabeth could probably have tolerated the missionaries. English Catholics were clearly loyal and, while recusancy might never be eliminated, it could at least be controlled and financially exploited. Opinion shifted dramatically when Edmund Campion and Robert Parsons landed in 1580. What happened?

▶ They organised a series of gentry safe-houses (to avoid charges of vagrancy and easy detection).
▶ They did not advise their charges to disobey Elizabeth's authority.
▶ Campion was an effective propagandist and sharp disputant.

On the other hand:

▶ by remaining largely in the south, they failed to have much of an impact in the north and in Wales (where they could have expected much greater support);

▶ they transcended the traditional English hierarchical structures (answering only to the Pope);

▶ they were resented (by the missionaries as interlopers and by the remaining Marian priests as foreigners);

▶ they worked effectively only with other Jesuits;

▶ they were seen as pro-Spanish (having been founded by a Spaniard).

The appearance of two distinct (and mutually hostile) types of priests effectively split and weakened the Catholic community. This, and other ideas we have discussed, also explains why the Armada generated so little domestic support.

But the final straw came in 1598 when the Pope decided to appoint a leader for the English Catholics. His choice of George Blackwell (a Jesuit) as 'Archpriest' forced many of the missionaries to appeal to Rome against him (thus becoming known as the 'Appellants'.) A particularly fierce pamphlet debate ensued between the Catholic groups, until the missionaries appealed to Elizabeth to rid England of the Jesuits. Too late, in 1602, the Pope agreed to make changes to the Archpriest's authority. Thus, by the last year of the Tudor period, Catholicism was little more than a hard-core minority sect, just about what Elizabeth hoped it would become all along.

Assessing Elizabethan reforms

Generally speaking, Elizabeth was successful. She had wanted to establish a broadly-based church, one that could accommodate as many of her subjects as possible, one that would make conformity as easy as possible. It also had to appeal to Protestants (in doctrine, scriptural and preaching terms) and Catholics (in ritual and hierarchical terms). By 1603, this is approximately what she had:

▶ a Protestant church with a Catholic structure
▶ one doctrinally Calvinist and ceremonially Catholic.

Moreover, by 1603, 'Roman' Catholicism was dying out, as was Puritan radicalism. True, the bishops' powers had been weakened, but at least they were still there in support of the supremacy.

TUTORIAL

Summary of key ideas
▶ **Alb** – the long white vestment wore by priests during religious ceremonies.

▶ **Cope** – the long cloak-like garment wore by priests and bishops during religious ceremonies.

▶ **Surplice** – the loose, white garment (reaching to the knee) worn over other garments by priests at services.

▶ **The rood** – a crucifix raised on a beam or on a screen at the entrance to the chancel (that part of the church near the altar reserved for the clergy).

▶ **Prophesying** – informal gatherings of like-minded Puritans, for the purpose of preaching, assessment of would-be preachers, and for the discussion of biblical passages and other issues.

▶ **Recusant(-s, -cy)** – those Catholics who could not or would not conform to the settlement and attend an established church.

▶ **Puritan(-s, -ism)** – a term of abuse describing those Protestants who wanted to see the elimination of all 'popish' or non-scriptural innovations from the established church.

▶ **Conformists** – those Puritans who came to realise that reform would proceed no further and who, consequently, made their peace with the settlement (as opposed to non-conformists, who could not settle down).

▶ **Presbyterians** – those Puritans who wished to see a Geneva-like settlement, particularly the elimination of bishops and priests in exchange for ministers, preachers, deacons and elders.

▶ **Separatists** – those who finally gave up and strove for the establishment of a completely separate 'Puritan' church.

Progress questions
1.   Why did the church need to be 'settled'?

2.   What was the ultimate influence of Mary Stuart?

Discussion points
1.   Why do historians consider Elizabeth a moderate Protestant?

2.   Why did Elizabeth place so little emphasis on theology and so much on tradition?

3.   Why did native Catholics fail to support schemes against Elizabeth?

Practical assignment
You will probably encounter 'challenge-type' questions (for example, 'Elizabeth successfully balanced the church between Protestant and Catholic extremes' – do you agree or disagree, and why?). To prepare, make a chart of three columns, listing the Protestant and Catholic demands and the Elizabethan solutions to help you decide.

Study and revision tips
You might well be asked to write about the settlement in an essay or on an exam. With this in mind, you should:

1.   Create a chronological outline of the main events (c.1558–1603) with some commentary on the motivations of the main figures involved (Elizabeth, Parker, Grindal, Whitgift, Mary Stuart, the Duke of Norfolk, etc.).

2.   Create a thematic outline of reign, divided by the main events (c.1558–1603) with a commentary on continuity between them, on the problems raised and on the solutions tried (the settlement, Puritan activism, Catholic plots, acts of parliament, propaganda, etc.).

Conclusion

One-minute summary – The Tudor Reformation was neither a single event (rather, a series of smaller, interconnected ones), nor was it exclusively religious in nature (having clear political, economic and social ramifications). Over the Tudor period we witness a religious revolution – unity (of people, church and practices), through a series of shifting diversities (radical Protestant experiments and reactionary Catholic retrenchment), back to unity (an all-embracing church, a traditionalist laity unconcerned by dogmatic purity). This conclusion will help you to understand:

▶ what really changed
▶ how to access the changes.

What really changed?

Religion, of course, in terms of doctrine but, more importantly, convictions changed. Prior to the 1530s, the Church in England (one part of a Rome-based international order) provided the people and their leaders with what they deemed necessary – from spiritual salvation to convenient common political and diplomatic grounds with the rest of Europe (and all things between); in other words, stability and unity. Post-1530s, this no longer seemed to be the case and the means to recapture stability and unity became the focus of each régime, each learning from, building upon or tearing down the work of the last. Elizabeth finally found stability and unity via a Church of England that combined elements from both old and new in a novel way.

Assessing the changes under Henry VIII

It was Henry's need for a 'divorce' – and the dynastic threat this implied – which eventually brought the Roman Catholic edifice crashing to the ground. Henry, good Catholic and Defender of the Faith though he was, had been forced to pursue other options, not only to secure the dynasty but to stabilise domestic conditions too. I leave it to you to assess motivations and assign blame.

What did Henry do?

In essence, Henry changed the structure of religion in England to suit his own needs (while only really tinkering with doctrine).

▶ He became 'supreme head' in order to draw the entire religious structure into his power and save the dynasty from collapse.

- ▶ He questioned papal doctrines and laws and found some wanting.

- ▶ He questioned whether the continued existence of monasteries, monks and nuns was really necessary (and found no compelling arguments in favour – indeed, the secularisation of former monastic resources strengthened the state).

- ▶ He left the traditional hierarchy of bishops and priests intact (because stability and unity demanded it).

- ▶ He kept some well-loved rites, ceremonies and traditional orthodoxies (sacraments, priestly authority, etc.) as common religious beliefs, structures and practices held a nation of increasingly divergent interests together.

So, if the Henrician Catholic Church was not all that dissimilar to its Roman precursor, a revolution once begun is impossible to stop. Henry succeeded (in that he got what he needed), kept things from going too far, but had opened the floodgates. Thus, by 1547, going back was unthinkable.

Assessing the changes under Edward VI
Under Edward, the revolution gained momentum – for good or ill. Some did not want to lose what gains they made previously; others (former exiles) had a vision.

- ▶ There were no priests in Geneva.
- ▶ Everybody was equally a priest in Wittenberg.

Edward's regents tried to control these desperate visions, which, when combined with the needs of the crown for stability and unity, led ultimately, to the demise of radicalism.

What did Edward do?
The political élites tried to force the revolution toward their own ends. Seymour took a moderate, rather subtle approach.

- ▶ Catholic relics and images were removed on the quiet.
- ▶ Reading of the Bible in English was encouraged.
- ▶ Chantries were dissolved.
- ▶ Priests were allowed to marry.

Seymour wanted to appease everyone. Security and unity would be ensured by a book and an act of parliament, neither of which were particularly radical. Thus:

- ▶ the people would slowly begin to see that Protestantism was not heresy
- ▶ as few Catholics as possible would suffer
- ▶ the aristocracy would continue to support reform.

Sadly, his message was lost in political ineptitude and unfulfilled expectations. Dudley, to forestall total collapse, took a more radical approach:

▶ altars (at the east end) were replaced with communion tables (in the centre);

▶ a more manifestly Protestant Prayer Book was introduced;

▶ long-held beliefs (like transubstantiation) and the more familiar visual aspects of religion (like clerical garb) were abandoned;

but it was too fast, too obviously political and a still largely Catholic population rejected it.

Assessing the changes under Mary
Devoted Catholic that she was, she saw the widespread support for her reign as a demand for complete religious reversal and, in pursuance, went too far.

What did Mary do?
She achieved almost all of her aims, but not as intended.

▶ All reforming statutes from the previous 20 years had been annulled (but few monasteries were restored).

▶ She achieved a marriage tie to the Habsburgs (but it was neither popular nor successful).

▶ She reinstalled papal obedience (but could not replace all Protestant clergy with Catholics, nor avoid rabid persecutions, nor convince anyone that theology *per se* still mattered).

Significantly, she could not deny the fact that the previous 20 years had had some impact and, by pretending otherwise she appeared tyrannical and as a dupe of foreign interlopers. Unconsciously perhaps, Mary undermined both stability and unity by her own hand.

Assessing the changes under Elizabeth
After some 30 years of religious strife, conflict and change, Elizabeth determined to settle the matter once and for all. By adopting a tolerant, but persuasive posture, she whittled away extreme positions and secured a religious settlement that was neither radical nor reactionary.

What did Elizabeth do?
In essence, Elizabeth brought the revolution around full circle. As in 1530, the church of England again provided the English with what they deemed necessary. It was a unique institution, combining both Calvinist and Catholic principles and

allowed for spiritual salvation and for convenient common political and diplomatic grounds upon which to build European alliances. Under Elizabeth, the English church, once again, provided stability and unity.

Sources

The following is a list of sources used and of further recommended readings in English (all published in London unless stated otherwise).

Introduction
Chibi, A. A., *The European Reformation (A student's guide to the key ideas and the events they shaped)* (Plymouth, 1999).
Cameron, A., *The European Reformation* (Oxford, 1991).
Elton, G. R., *England Under the Tudors* (1991, 3rd edn.).
Elton, G. R., *Reform and Reformation England, 1509–1558* (Harvard, 1977).
Greengrass, M., *The Longman Companion to the European Reformation c.1500–1618* (1998).
Duffy, E., *The Stripping of the Altars: Traditional Religion in England, c.1400–1580* (New Haven, 1992).
Guy, J., *Tudor England* (Oxford, 1988).
Scarisbrick, J. J., *The Reformation and the English People* (Oxford, 1984).
Fletcher, A. and MacCulloch, D., *Tudor Rebellions* (1997).

Chapter 1
Surtz, E. and Murphy, V. (eds.), *The Divorce Tracts of Henry VIII* (Angers, 1988).
Gwyn, P., *The King's Cardinal* (1990).
Ives, E., *Anne Boleyn* (Oxford, 1986).
Kelly, H. A., *The Matrimonial Trials of Henry VIII* (Stanford, 1976).
Murphy, V., 'The Literature and Propaganda of Henry VIII's First Divorce', in *The Reign of Henry VIII. Politics, Policy and Piety*, ed. D. MacCulloch (New York, 1995). *Calender of State Papers (CSP)*.
Scarisbrick, J.J., *Henry VIII* (1968)
Warnicke, R. M., *The Rise and Fall of Anne Boleyn* (Cambridge, 1991 edn.)
Marius, R., *Thomas More* (New York, 1985)
Chibi, A. A., *Henry VIII's Conservative Scholar: Bishop John Stokesley and the Divorce, Royal Supremacy and Doctrinal Reform* (Bern, 1997).

Chapter 2
Bowker, M., 'The Supremacy and the Episcopate: The Struggle for Control, 1534–1540', *Historical Journal* xviii:2 (1975).
Doernberg, E., *Henry VIII and Luther* (1961).
Knowles, D., *The Religious Orders in England* (3 vols., Cambridge, 1959).
Lehmberg, S. E., *The Reformation Parliament 1529–1536* (Cambridge, 1970).
Lehmberg, S. E., *The Later Parliaments of Henry VIII: 1536–1547* (Cambridge, 1977).

MacCulloch, D., *Thomas Cranmer: A Life* (New Haven, 1996).

O'Grady, P., *Henry VIII and the Conforming Catholics* (Collegeville, Minn., 1990).

Woodward, G. W. O., *Dissolution of the Monasteries* (1966).

Randell, K., *Henry VIII and the Reformation in England* (1993).

Rex, R., *Henry VIII and the English Reformation* (1993).

Hoyle, R. W., 'The Origins of the dissolution of the monasteries', *Historical Journal* xxxviii:ii (June 1995).

Chapter 3

Jordan, W.K., *Edward VI: The Young King (The Protectorship of the Duke of Somerset)* (1968).

Jordan, W.K., *Edward VI: The Threshold of Power (The Dominance of the Duke of Northumberland)* (1970).

Williams, P., *The Later Tudors: England 1547–1603* (1995).

Loach, J., *Edward VI*, G. Bernard and P. Williams (eds.) (1999).

Beer, B. L. *Northumberland: The Political Career of John Dudley, Earl of Warwick and Duke of Northumberland* (Kent, 1973).

Jones, W. R. D., *The Mid-Tudor Crisis*, 1539–1563 (1973).

Loach, J., *Protector Somerset: A Reassessment* (Bangor, 1994).

Loades, J., *John Dudley, Duke of Northumberland, 1504–1553* (Oxford, 1996).

Loades, J., *The Mid-Tudor Crisis, 1545–1565* (1992).

Ridley, J., *Nicholas Ridley: A Biography* (1957).

Chapter 4

Heard, N., *Edward VI and Mary: A Mid-Tudor Crisis?* (1990)

Tittler, R., *The Reign of Mary I* (1991)

Erickson, C., *Bloody Mary* (New York, 1978)

Loach, J., *Parliament and the Crown in the Reign of Mary Tudor* (Oxford, 1986)

Loades, D., *Mary Tudor, a life* (1989)

Loades, D., *The Reign of Mary Tudor, Politics, Government and Religion in England, 1553–58* (1979)

Parker, G., *Phillip II* (1978).

Chapter 5

Collinson, P., *Archbishop Grindal* (1979).

Collinson, P., *English Puritanism* (1983).

Collinson, P., *The Elizabethan Puritan Movement* (1967).

MacCaffrey, W., *Elizabeth I* (1993).

Foster, A., *The Church of England 1570–1640* (1994).

Acheson, R. J., *Radical Puritans in England, 1550–1660* (1990).

Haigh, C. (ed), *The Reign of Elizabeth I* (1984).

Jones, N. L., *Faith by Statute: Parliament and the Settlement of Religion 1559* (1982).

Lake, P., *Moderate Puritans and the Elizabethan Church* (Cambridge, 1982).

Lake, P., Anglicans and Puritans? (1988).

Warren, J., *Elizabeth I: Religion and Foreign Affairs* (1993).

Doran, S., *Elizabeth I and Religion 1558–1603* (1994).

Conclusion

Loach, J., *Parliament under the Tudors* (Oxford, 1991).

Cross, C., *Church and People* (1976).

Doran, S. and Durstan, C., *Princes, Pastors and People: The Church and Religion in England, 1529–1689* (1991).

MacCulloch, D., *The Later Reformation in England, 1547–1603* (1990).

Bernard, G., 'The Church of England c.1529–c.1642', *History* 75 (1990).

Haigh, C., *English Reformations: Religion, Politics and Society Under the Tudors* (Oxford, 1993).

Websites for Tudor Reformation Studies

The world wide web is a very useful resource, giving the history student nearly free and almost immediate information on any topic. Ignore this valuable store of materials at your peril! However great it is, though, it is no substitute for honest research. The following list of websites was created as a guide that may be helpful for further readings on:

- ▶ primary documents (like books)
- ▶ secondary sources (like academic papers)
- ▶ visual aids (like maps, buildings, portraits).

http://www.tudorhistory.org
Although this is a rather basic site with regard to information on the various aspects of reformation, it does feature a comprehensive selection of visual aids, including portraits, busts, coinage, masks and architectural features of Tudor places of interests. There are plans for expansion.

http://cts.bvm.com.au/australia/acts1198.html
This is a rather old, but still useful and interesting, if somewhat negative, essay on the Reformation-related works of Mary I. It is the M.A. thesis of D G M Jackson, as published by the Catholic Truth Society.

http://www.britainexpress.com/History/Dissolution_of_the_monasteries.htm
A basic examination of the dissolutions, featuring textbooks, and a searchable archive of persons and social events involved. It is worth exploring for short articles on Henry VIII, Wolsey, Cranmer, Monasteries, the Pilgrimage of Grace, Edward VI, Mary, Elizabeth and a more general examination of the Tudor church can all be found.

http://infoplease.lycos.com/ce6/people/A0866810.html
This site features a search engine. The essay on Henry VIII provides a number of jumping-off points, including one very good one to Katherine of Aragon, and other basic but interesting sub-essays. One could spend hours gainfully searching this resource.

http://awylie.tripod.com/english.htm
A useful essay on the English Reformation (which is used as a jumping-off point to other areas of related interest. One leads to a source of interesting essays about Henry VIII. This is a useful site and a good place to start essay research.

http://www.sscnet.ucla.edu/history/graduate/euroexam/brithist.htm
This site offers an extensive and useful bibliography.

http://www.scionofzion.com/marytudor.htm
A useful, readable, but short essay on the reign of Mary by Sylvia Lacoshi.

http://www.geocities.com/historicom/Tudor.htm
A good, readable essay written by Owen Mulpetre. The site features several good pictures and a useful bibliography for further research.

http://web.uvic.ca/shakespeare/Library/SLT/fset_whole.htm?page=henryviii.book=ideas
This is the jump point to a primary document written by Thomas Cranmer.

http://www.rjtarr.freeserve.co.uk/Miscellaneous/hotpots/earlybritish/henryviii/refcross-word.htm
Something to break up the monotony a little, this crossword puzzle is rather difficult and will test your general Tudor knowledge.

http://www.gospelcom.net/chi/HERITAGF/Issuenos/ch1021.shtml
This is an electronic copy of *The King's Book*. It features a facsimile frontispiece and a jump point to the Christian Heritage Library. A useful primary source.

http://www.geocities.com/seemag1/henryviii/links.html
A useful and extensive jumping-off point to a number of useful sites about Henry VIII, including a portrait gallery, a landscapes gallery and others.

http://www.geocities.com/CollegePark/2809 which is 'Clare's Tudor Page'.
This one features a searchable bridge to other galleries and several basic essays on many aspects of the Tudor period. Interesting, but of limited value to reformation specific searches.

http://rc.net/%7Eerasmus/RAZ75.htm
This site features a vast selection of secondary source quotations on various aspects of the Henrician Reformation period.

http://www.luminarium.org/renlist/tudor.htm
This site features some primary sources, although it is rather limited with regard to the Reformation.

http://www.royal.gov.uk/history/tudor
This site is a good jumping off point to a number of specific essays and picture archives.

http://www.canonlaw.anglican.org/1549ActUni.htm
This is an electronic version of the first Act of Uniformity of Edward VI; a very useful primary resource. The home page of this site might be usefully explored, although there seems to be few other relevant sources.

http://www.thehistorychannel.co.uk/classroom/alevel/reformation1.htm
A very interesting and useful article by Diamaid MacCulloch that features a good explanation of the various doctrines examined throughout the English Reformation period. It also looks at the people and events involved. There is a useful connection to a portrait gallery and a selection of brief biographies. Certainly worth the time it takes to explore it fully.

http://www.seanet.com/~eldrbarry/heidel/englrsc.htm
A good start point to a selection of downloadable materials like timelines, biographies and examinations of events and is certainly worth some exploration. I was particularly impressed with *www.apostles.com/johnfisher.html*; a no less than brilliant little page.

Index